CONTENTS

TOPIC 1 FOOD AND HEALTH

Unit 1   Food   2
Unit 2   Carbohydrates   4
Unit 3   Proteins   6
Unit 4   Fats   8
Unit 5   Energy values of food   10
Unit 6   Vitamins and minerals, water and fibre   13
Unit 7   Digestion and the digestive system   16
Unit 8   Eating disorders   19
Unit 9   Child obesity – are fad diets the answer?   21

TOPIC 2 EVERYDAY ELEMENTS AND COMPOUNDS

Unit 10   Elements, compounds and mixtures   24
Unit 11   Separating mixtures   27
Unit 12   Atoms, elements and the Periodic Table   30
Unit 13   Compounds   32
Unit 14   Oxygen – the element of life   34
Unit 15   Hydrogen – an explosive element   36
Unit 16   Carbon dioxide – fizz and foam   38
Unit 17   Plastics – the material of our time   41

TOPIC 3 ENERGY ALL AROUND US

Unit 18   What is energy?   44
Unit 19   Forms of energy   46
Unit 20   Energy transferred and transformed   49
Unit 21   Efficiency and power   52
Unit 22   The energy of food   55
Unit 23   Non-renewable energy sources   58
Unit 24   Energy for the future – renewable energy sources   61
Unit 25   An example of alternative energy production in New Zealand   63

TOPIC 4 OUT OF THIS WORLD

Unit 26   The third rock from the sun   65
Unit 27   The Moon – Earth's natural satellite   68
Unit 28   Space Exploration – inner planets of Venus and Mars   71
Unit 29   Space exploration – outer planets of Jupiter, Saturn, Neptune, Uranus   74
Unit 30   Satellites   76
Unit 31   GPS – Global Positioning System   78
Unit 32   Space travel – living in space   80
Unit 33   Space spin-offs   82

Answers   Removable section in the centre of the book
Glossary   84

UNIT 01 FOOD

The diets of animals vary greatly. So does the way they get their food. For example:

- tapeworms lie in their food in the host's intestine and absorb food through their body walls
- aphids suck plant sap
- sea urchins (kina) graze on algae growing on rocks
- snakes swallow small animals whole
- humpback whales, using large brush-like plates called baleen, strain krill and small fish from the water
- cows chew grass.

Animals cannot make their own food as plants do in photosynthesis. Animals must get the chemicals they need to grow and survive, by eating 'food' (plant material and other animals). This is why they are called consumers.

Herbivores such as cows, sheep, caterpillars and earthworms eat plant material.

Carnivores such as frogs, sharks, spiders and hawks eat meat (other animals).

Omnivores such as humans, pigs, bears and cockroaches eat both plant material and meat.

Some people choose to be vegetarians. They eat only plant material although some also eat dairy products such as eggs, milk, butter and cheese.

The strictest vegetarians are called vegans. They eat no meat or animal products.

Food is necessary for:

- energy for all the different types of work the body has to do
- growth – making new cells and replacing old ones
- mending damaged tissue
- warmth
- keeping healthy.

Animals need different types of food for different purposes. The different food groups are:

- carbohydrates e.g. sugars and starches
- proteins e.g. meats, dairy food and nuts
- fats e.g. butter, cheese and olive oil
- vitamins and minerals.

Animals also need water and fibre in their diets.

1 Give the names of

a) 2 herbivores not named in the unit _____

b) 2 carnivores not named in the unit _____

c) 1 omnivore not named in the unit _____

d) 3 non-meat dairy products that people eat _____

e) the 4 main food groups needed in a balanced diet _____

2 Use ticks to show which foods the 6 groups eat.

	HAM	BUTTER	leaf	eggs	algae	cheese	BRAZIL NUTS
kina							
herbivore							
vegetarian							
cockroach							
omnivore							
vegan							

3 Fill out the thought bubbles to show the difference food can make.

No energy.

Gash won't heal.

Brrh! I'm so cold!

Can't shake this 'flu.

4 Suggest sources of protein for vegetarians or vegans.

_____

_____

5 Write down 3 things you have learned from this unit.

a) _____

b) _____

c) _____

6 Write down anything you need to ask your teacher to explain.

_____

Carbohydrates come in **2** different types – **sugars** and **starches**.
They are used in the body to produce energy.

Sugars are called simple carbohydrates. This is because your body digests them quickly and easily. Simple carbohydrates are usually sweet tasting, like biscuits, lollies, soft drinks, and other sugary foods. Fruits also contain simple carbohydrates.

Starchy carbohydrates are called complex carbohydrates because they take longer to be digested than do simple carbohydrates. Complex carbohydrates are found in foods like bread, noodles, rice, and many vegetables such as potatoes and kumara.

Carbohydrates have an important job. They give all the cells in your body the energy they need. When you eat foods with carbohydrates in them, your body breaks them down into two different types of fuel.

Type 1 For energy that you will use right away, your body turns carbohydrates into **glucose**. Glucose is carried in your blood to all the cells in your body. It gives you energy. Whatever you do, even something as simple as writing in your science book, you need the energy of glucose.

Type 2 But your cells can use only so much glucose at one time. So when there is glucose left over that cannot be used right away, it is stored in your liver and muscles as a substance called **glycogen**. The glycogen that does not fit into your liver and muscle cells is turned into **fat** and stored in your body. Glycogen can be released for fast energy when you are doing something like sprinting or another quick exercise. But if you are exercising for a long time, your body uses its stored fat.

Simple carbohydrates, especially sugars, are in many foods. They supply energy quickly. But they can often come with lots of fat and lack important vitamins that your body needs. However, many fruits are a good source of simple carbohydrates. So if you are looking for some quick energy and a healthy snack, try bananas, dates, kiwifruit and pineapple. These carbohydrates have a high Glycemic Index (a number that compares them to glucose, one of the fastest carbohydrates available; its GI [Glycemic Index] = 100). They provide energy quickly for a brief time.

Complex carbohydrates found in foods like bread, cereal, rice and pasta give you energy more slowly. This is because they take longer to be digested. They are better when you are exercising for a long time or playing in a game. This is because they will supply energy over a longer period of time. Complex carbohydrates usually come with lots of vitamins and minerals that your body needs e.g. in corn, potatoes, tomatoes, carrots. These carbohydrates have a low glycemic index compared to glucose and provide energy over a longer period of time.

Cellulose is a carbohydrate found in the walls of plant cells. It is the main component in wood. Like starch, cellulose is made of glucose molecules. But they are linked together in a different way to form tough fibres. Humans can not digest or break down cellulose. It provides the fibre in our diets, keeping our digestive system healthy, but providing no energy-giving nutrients. Herbivores like cows and sheep that live on grass and other plant material have bacteria living in their guts. The bacteria can break down cellulose and release its energy for the animals to use.

1 Give reasons for the following.

a) **We need to eat carbohydrates.** _____

b) **Marathon runners often have a large pasta meal the night before they are going to run.**

_____

c) **We need to eat fruit and vegetables (plant material) even though we cannot digest the cellulose they contain.**

   (2 reasons) _____

2 Write either simple or complex under each food to show if it is a simple or complex carbohydrate.

a)	b)	c)	d)	e)	f)

3 Explain what glycogen is. _____

4 Think about what you have eaten in the past 24 hours. List:

a) **3 sugary foods you have eaten.** _____

b) **3 starchy foods you have eaten.** _____

5 Name 2 healthy, energy-giving snacks you could eat when you get home from school.

(1) _____   (2) _____

6 Beside the following GI write what it tells you about how quickly these foods provide you with energy.

a) **dates = 103** _____

b) **spaghetti = 44** _____

7 Write down 3 things you have learned from this unit.

a) _____

b) _____

c) _____

8 Write down anything you need to ask your teacher to explain.

_____

UNIT 03 PROTEINS

Proteins are the building blocks of our bodies.

Proteins have an important role in everything we do.

Proteins are really a combination of many smaller chemicals called **amino acids**. There are 20 different amino acids that can combine in lots of ways to make thousands of different proteins (just as the 26 letters of our alphabet combine to make all the words in the dictionary).

There are 11 non-essential amino acids. You make these inside your body. You need them to keep your body healthy. But they are not essential as part of the food you eat.

There are 9 essential amino acids. These must come from eating foods with protein in them. They give your body the amino acids needed to make the proteins your body must have to grow and to work properly.

Protein is used to build up, maintain, and replace the tissues in your body. It is what helps make your cuts and scrapes heal. Your muscles, skin and hair are made up mostly of protein. The silk that spiders spin is also protein. So is the horn of a rhinoceros.

Protein helps your body in other ways too:

Transport: Red blood cells contain a protein called haemoglobin that carries oxygen around the body.

Defence: Antibodies, the cells that fight off infection and disease.

Messenger: Hormones (chemical messengers in your body).

Chemical reactions: Enzymes (special proteins) control all the reactions in cells.

It is easy to get the protein your body needs. Protein is in foods like meat, chicken, fish, eggs, nuts, and dairy products like cheese, milk, and yoghurt, and in beans and lentils.

Not everyone is lucky enough to have a diet rich in protein. New Zealanders do because farming means meat and dairy products are cheaply and readily available.

Kwashiorkor is a disease common among children in tropical Africa. It is due to a lack of protein. Once mothers stop breast feeding their children, they start feeding them on starchy carbohydrate foods. Those foods do not supply the nutritional needs of growing children. Children with kwashiorkor have no energy to play or move about. Some can not even feed themselves. Their physical and mental development is badly affected. Because they can not make antibodies to fight disease, they catch infections easily. They often die before they are five-years-old. Children with kwashiorkor do not look like they are suffering from malnutrition. They have round faces. Their arms and legs might appear well-padded. Their abdomens poke out. This is because without protein in their blood, fluid collects in their tissues. Their bodies become water-logged. But they can be treated. Firstly they are given milk that has vitamins and minerals added. Then they must be fed a normal balanced diet with enough protein to meet their needs.

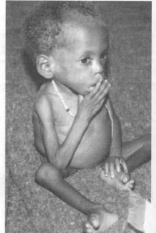

1 Around the drawing, list the key ways protein is used in the body.

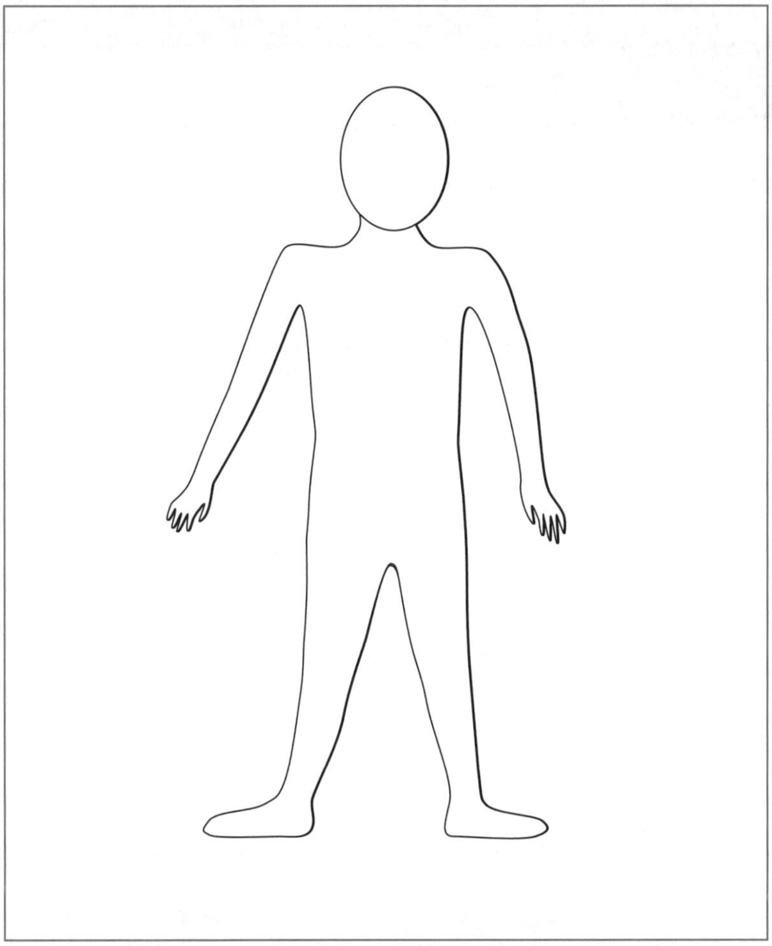

2 Name 3 protein foods that you have eaten over the past 24 hours.

a) _____

b) _____

c) _____

3 Give answers to these questions.

a) What is happening to the bodies of children that makes it so important that they get enough protein in their daily

diet? _____

b) Why do New Zealand children get plenty of protein in their daily diets? _____

c) Why is breast milk better for young children than a starchy diet? _____

d) How could countries like New Zealand help countries where kwashiorkor is still a big problem?

_____

4 Write down what the following numbers have to do with protein.

11	9

5 Write down 3 things you have learned from this unit.

a) _____

b) _____

c) _____

6 Write down anything you need to ask your teacher to explain.

_____

UNIT 04 | FATS

Fat is the body's major form of energy storage. When they are broken down, fats give more than twice the energy of carbohydrates.

Many fats that people eat are really a combination of two different types of substances: saturated fats and unsaturated fats.

Saturated fats

- They are in most animal fats such as meat, milk, cheese, butter.
- Having a large amount of saturated fats in the diet has been linked to high levels of 'bad' cholesterol in the blood. This in turn can lead to blocked blood vessels, high blood pressure and heart attacks.

Unsaturated fats

- They are mostly in plant oils such as olive oil and corn oil.
- Replacing saturated fats with unsaturated fats can help reduce levels of 'bad' cholesterol in the blood and reduce the risks of heart attack and heart disease.

As well as providing your body with energy, fats also:

- insulate your body from the cold and give some protection for your organs.
- help to make up important hormones that you need to keep your body at the right temperature or keep your blood pressure at the right level.
- help give you healthy skin and hair.
- help store vitamins A, D, E, and K, and transport them through your bloodstream when your body needs them.

Your body needs some fat to work properly. But most people eat more fat than they need. Eating a lot of fatty foods such as cakes, chocolate, fast food hamburgers and fries, can contribute to obesity (when a person weighs much too much for his or her height). It can also contribute to other illnesses when you are older, like heart disease or diabetes.

1 Some fat questions for you:

a) Name 3 fatty foods that you have eaten in the past 24 hourrs.

i) _____ ii) _____ iii) _____

b) Say why you need to have some fat in your diet. _____

_____

c) Say what types of fats you should have in your diet. _____

_____

d) Name some foods that contain this type of fat. _____

_____

2 Write down the words in the unit that show:

a) how much more energy fats give than carbohydrates. _____

b) examples of foods that can contribute to obesity. _____

c) what may help reduce bad cholesterol in the blood. _____

d) the 5 things that fats do for your body. _____

3 Give the answers to the following 'What Am I's?'

I am the type of fat that could help give you a very bad cholesterol reading.
a) _____

I am your body's main form of energy storage.
b) _____

I am the overweight condition you could get if you ate too much fat.
c) _____

I am the type of fat that is the kindest to your body.
d) _____

I am the form food is in when it gives more than twice the energy of carbohydrates.
e) _____

4 Write down 3 things you have learned from this unit.

a) _____

b) _____

c) _____

5 Write down anything you need to ask your teacher to explain.

_____

UNIT 05 ENERGY VALUES OF FOOD

A kilojoule is a measure of how much energy the food you eat can supply your body. When you eat food, your body uses the food as fuel to produce energy. 1 kilojoule = 1,000 joules. (Food energy values used to be measured in calories.)

Some types of food provide more kilojoules of energy than others. Fats provide twice as much energy as carbohydrates do.

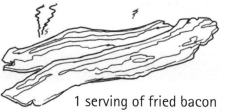

1 serving of cornflakes and milk = 630kJ

1 serving of fried bacon = 1300kJ

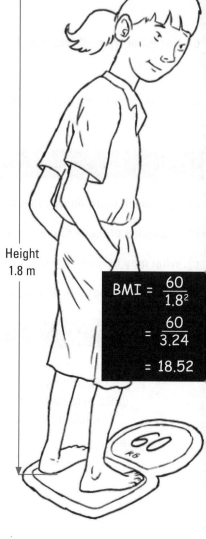

Height 1.8 m

$$BMI = \frac{60}{1.8^2}$$
$$= \frac{60}{3.24}$$
$$= 18.52$$

Since fats give more energy than other food types, you might think that eating a lot of fatty foods would be good for you. It is not. Your body can use only so much energy at one time. Whatever it does not use, it stores in your body as fat. This can lead to obesity and other health problems.

The key to keeping your body healthy is to remember that your body uses food for energy. When you are active, playing soccer or swimming for example, your body burns lots of energy. When you are watching TV or playing on the computer, your body does not burn nearly as much energy.

To keep your body at a weight that is in proportion to (good for) your height, eat as much food as you need to provide the energy you use in your daily life. The more active you are the more you can eat. It is still a good idea to get most of your energy from carbohydrates. Fat will not hurt you if you eat it but it should make up a little less than 1/3 of all the kilojoules you eat.

It is widely believed that young teenagers should eat enough food to supply their bodies with 10,000–15,000 kilojoules of energy per day. However, many things such as age, sex, the work a person does, daily activity and body size, have an effect on how many kilojoules a person needs.

In healthy women the normal amount of body weight stored as fat is 20–25%. In healthy men it is 15–19%. Obesity is often the result of eating more food than your body uses in a day.

A person's level of obesity can be measured through the body mass index (BMI). It is measured by the following equation:

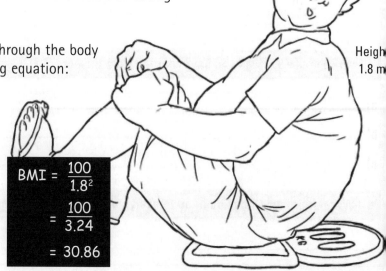

Height 1.8 m

$$BMI\ (kg/m^2) = \frac{weight\ (kg)}{(height\ (m))^2}$$

A person's BMI can fit into one of these ranges:

- less than 20 is underweight
- 20 to 25 is desirable weight
- 25 to 30 is overweight
- over 30 is obese
- over 35 is very obese.

$$BMI = \frac{100}{1.8^2}$$
$$= \frac{100}{3.24}$$
$$= 30.86$$

Dieting or limiting food intake for a short time in order to lose weight is rarely successful in the long term and can be harmful. A lifestyle of healthy eating and exercise is more likely to be sustainable over a long period of time. Teenagers need to be careful because their bodies are still growing. Dieting may stop their bodies getting the nutrients they need. When you diet, your body responds by using energy more slowly, so it is harder to lose weight. The body may also start to use muscle protein as a source of energy. So weight loss is not due to using up fat, but using up important protein.

A healthy diet should include a wide variety of different foods with plenty of fruit and vegetables and not too much fat or added sugar. A portion is about as much food as you can hold in the palm of your hand.

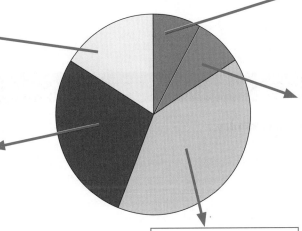

Protein foods such as meat, fish, eggs, beans, nuts: You should eat 2 portions a day.

Milk and dairy foods: You should eat at least 1 portion a day for the calcium and vitamins they contain.

Starchy foods such as bread, cereals, pasta and rice should form a large part of each meal.

Sugary and fatty foods such as sweets, potato chips, fizzy drinks, fried foods and pies: You should eat only 1 portion a day.

Fruit and vegetables: You should eat at least 5 portions a day.

4 U 2 D O

1   Give answers to these questions.

a) **What part of food do we measure using kilojoules?** _____

b) **How many joules are in a kilojoule?** _____

c) **What does your body do with excess energy?** _____

2   You are going to be running the cross country course at school.

a) **Would you be better to have bacon or cornflakes for breakfast?** _____

b) **Give a reason for your answer.** _____

3   Complete the diagram about BMI.

BMI Range/Bodyweight Description

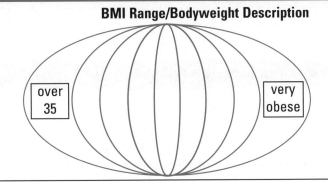

over 35

very obese

4 Your BMI

a) Use the formula given to calculate your body mass index. _____

b) Write down if you are the desirable weight for your height. _____

5 Think about the activities you do during a week and write

a) on which days you should eat more food and why. _____

_____

_____

b) on which days you should eat less food and why. _____

_____

_____

6 Your food

a) Write a list of the food you ate yesterday. _____

_____

_____

_____

b) Write whether you ate the correct portions of each type of food. _____

c) Write which foods you ate too much of. _____

_____

_____

_____

d) Write which foods you did not eat enough of. _____

_____

_____

_____

7 Write down 3 things you have learned from this unit.

a) _____

b) _____

c) _____

8 Write down anything you need to ask your teacher to explain.

_____

_____

UNIT 06 VITAMINS AND MINERALS, WATER AND FIBRE

Vitamins are:

- organic (carbon-containing) substances
- essential for healthy bodies
- involved in chemical reactions that take place in your cells
- needed by your body only in small amounts each day
- supplied by a healthy balanced diet without the need of vitamin supplements.

Even though only small amounts are required, a lack or deficiency of vitamins can cause serious problems.

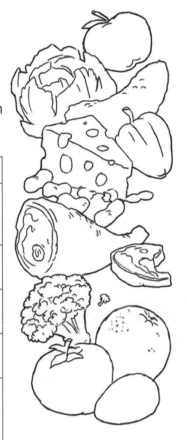

Vitamin	Food source	Deficiency disease
Vitamin A	dark green and orange vegetables and fruits, dairy products	night blindness (difficulty adapting to darkness); dry scaling skin
Vitamin B-1 (thiamine)	pork, peanuts, whole grains, egg yolk	beriberi – tired, loss of appetite, weakness
Vitamin B-2 (riboflavin)	meat, dairy products, vegetables	skin lesions such as cracks at corner of mouth
Vitamin C	fruit especially citrus fruit, broccoli, tomato	scurvy – loose teeth, bleeding gums, bruise easily, wounds slow to heal
Vitamin D	dairy products, egg yolk (also made in the human skin in presence of sunlight)	rickets – bone softening leading to deformity

Minerals are chemical elements other than carbon, hydrogen, oxygen and nitrogen that are found in organic compounds. Several are necessary in our diet for the healthy functioning of our bodies. But they are needed only in small amounts. Like vitamins, the lack of any of the essential minerals can cause deficiency diseases.

Mineral	Source	Use in body	Lack causes
calcium (Ca)	dairy products (e.g. milk), dark green vegetables	building bones and teeth, blood clotting, muscle and nerve function	stunted growth, possibly rickets
iron (Fe)	meats, eggs, whole grains, green leafy vegetables	part of the protein haemoglobin in blood that carries oxygen	anaemia – weakness, pale, lacking energy
iodine (I)	seafood, iodised salt	part of thyroid hormones	goitre – an enlarged thyroid gland in the neck
fluorine (F)	drinking water, seafood, and tea	maintains tooth structure	more tooth decay

Water has no energy value. Yet we cannot survive more than a couple of days without it. All body cells, tissues and fluids contain water. In fact nearly 75% of our body weight is water. We need between 2 and 3 litres of water each day. We get about half the water we need from the food we eat. Nutritionists also recommend that we drink several glasses of water each day. In the body water is used for:

transport: Plasma makes up 55% of your blood and most of it is water. It carries digested food, hormones, heat, antibodies and wastes.

waste removal: Urine is 96% water and the rest is made up of a waste product called urea. Excess salts your body does not need and any harmful substances are also removed in urine.

temperature control: Sweat or perspiration is mostly water vapour. When it evaporates off our skin, it cools us down.

chemical reactions in our cells: Many substances dissolve in water. This makes it easier for reactions to take place.

Fibre or roughage is the name given to the cellulose part of plant material that humans cannot digest. It helps to keep the digestive system healthy by keeping the food moving along it. In carnivores such as lions, the hide (skin and hair) of the animals they eat acts as roughage to keep their digestive systems healthy.

4U2DO

1   Look at the chart about vitamins and answer these questions.

a) **What dark green vegetable would be a good source of Vitamin A?** _____

b) **What orange vegetable would be a good source of Vitamin A?** _____

c) **What orange fruit would be a good source of Vitamin A?** _____

d) **What foods could a vegetarian eat to supply their body with Vitamin B1? (thiamine)?** _____

_____

e) **What 3 different citrus fruits could you eat to get Vitamin C?** _____

f) **Why is Vitamin D also known as the sunshine Vitamin?** _____

2   Look at the chart about minerals and answer these questions.

a) **What dairy product, containing calcium, can you drink every day to give you strong bones and teeth?**

_____

b) **Why do people who suffer from anaemia, feel tired and lacking in energy?** _____

_____

c) **Why do teenage girls suffer from anaemia more than teenage boys?** _____

_____

d) **Why should you drink plenty of water each day?** _____

_____

e) **Why are breakfast cereals good sources of fibre?** _____

_____

3 Suggest reasons for the following.

a) In some zoos where animals are fed raw meat, the animals are also given horsehide occasionally.

_____

_____

b) Some people say vitamin supplements are nothing but expensive urine.

_____

_____

c) Captain Cook insisted his sailors have lime juice in their diet.

_____

_____

4 Name the disease each person is suffering and suggest foods the person should eat.

_____

_____

_____

_____

_____

_____

_____

_____

_____

_____

_____

_____

a)

b)

c)

d)

5 Write down 3 things you have learned from this unit.

a) _____

b) _____

c) _____

6 Write down anything you need to ask your teacher to explain.

_____

_____

The food that animals eat contains the chemicals they need to power all body activities, to build new cells and replace damaged ones. Before this can happen, the food has to be physically and chemically broken down. Then it has to be transported to the body's cells where the chemicals can be used.

This breakdown process occurs in **4** stages:

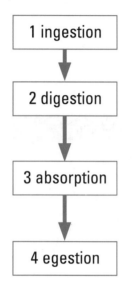

1 ingestion	the act of eating or getting food into the body (mouth)
2 digestion	enzymes break down the carbohydrates, proteins and fats into simple chemicals (stomach and duodenum)
3 absorption	the chemicals are absorbed into the bloodstream and transported to the body's cells where they are used (small intestine)
4 egestion	food that cannot be broken down (fibre) is passed out of the body (rectum/anus)

Processing the food into a useable form takes place in the digestive system. The food canal is one long tube from mouth to anus. It has specialised regions along the way to carry out the four stages of **ingestion**, **digestion**, **absorption** and **egestion**.

The regions vary in herbivores, carnivores and omnivores. This is because of the different types of food they process e.g. sheep have teeth to grind their food whereas earthworms and birds have a gizzard (a pouch-like organ) where their food is ground up.

Rhythmic muscle contractions push the food through the tube. Along the way, digestive glands add digestive juices containing enzymes to the food. This speeds up the chemical breakdown.

Enzymes are a special type of protein that work in the body to speed up chemical reactions. Digestive enzymes:

- break down carbohydrates, proteins and fats into simple chemicals that can be used in the body
- are made in special glands attached to the digestive system by short tubes
- work best at body temperature
- can be destroyed by heat.
- act on only one type of food.

Examples of ENZYMES

Amylase in saliva starts to break down starch.

Pepsin in the stomach begins the break down of protein.

Lipases in the duodenum break down fat molecules.

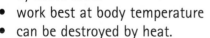

1 Draw arrows from each box to the correct parts of the body.

The human digestive system works like this:

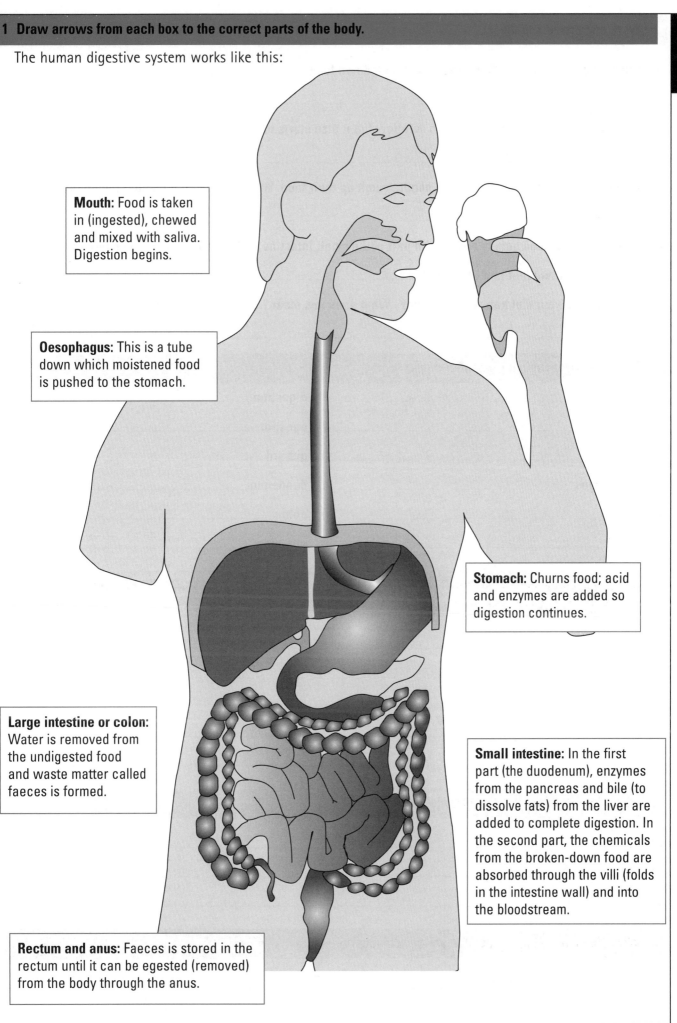

Mouth: Food is taken in (ingested), chewed and mixed with saliva. Digestion begins.

Oesophagus: This is a tube down which moistened food is pushed to the stomach.

Stomach: Churns food; acid and enzymes are added so digestion continues.

Large intestine or colon: Water is removed from the undigested food and waste matter called faeces is formed.

Small intestine: In the first part (the duodenum), enzymes from the pancreas and bile (to dissolve fats) from the liver are added to complete digestion. In the second part, the chemicals from the broken-down food are absorbed through the villi (folds in the intestine wall) and into the bloodstream.

Rectum and anus: Faeces is stored in the rectum until it can be egested (removed) from the body through the anus.

2 Work out answers to these.

a) What happens in the mouth to physically break down food? _____

_____

b) Saliva moistens food so it is easier to swallow but it also starts to chemically break down the food; so what must be in saliva to do this? _____

c) Sometimes, for a number of reasons, people vomit up their food. Why does vomit burn your mouth (and damage your teeth)? _____

d) By the time your food gets to the second part of the small intestine, it does not look anything like the food you put in your mouth. What is it like now? _____

e) Eating fibre in your diet keeps you 'regular'. What does this mean? _____

_____

3 Give a short meaning for the following.

a) ingestion _____ b) digestion _____

c) absorption _____ d) egestion _____

e) fibre _____ f) gizzard _____

g) oesophagus _____ h) duodenum _____

i) villi _____ j) colon _____

k) faeces _____ l) enzymes _____

4 Some washing powders claim to have 'hungry enzymes' in them to get rid of stains. Try to explain what must be happening in your washing machine for this to happen.

_____

_____

_____

_____

_____

5 Write down 3 things you have learned from this unit.

a) _____

b) _____

c) _____

6 Write down anything you need to ask your teacher to explain.

_____

_____

UNIT 08 EATING DISORDERS

Anorexia nervosa, bulimia nervosa and compulsive overeating are the 3 major eating disorders. Many doctors believe they are the result of emotional problems. There may also be a physical cause such as a hormone imbalance in the body.

Anorexia nervosa means loss of appetite for nervous reasons. People with anorexia will show some or all of these features:

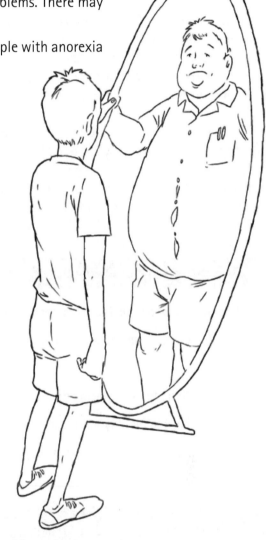

- deliberate refusal to gain weight, so their weight is far below the healthy minimum for their height
- fear of becoming fat
- intense desire to be thin
- warped view of their body shape
- in girls menstruation often stops
- vomiting, the use of laxatives (drugs that loosen the bowels), excessive exercise to get rid of food.

Anorexia is more common in females (about 90%) than males. Teenagers and people in their early 20s are most at risk. Severe weight loss (15–60% of body weight) is only one result of anorexia. Other physical symptoms can be:

- feeling weak and exhausted, having no energy
- feeling faint and dizzy
- feeling cold
- constipation and stomach pain
- bloated stomach, swollen face and/or ankles
- loss of head hair
- fine hair can start to grow on body
- in girls a drop in the levels of the hormone oestrogen causes menstruation to stop, and bones to thin
- early death (50% from suicide).

Bulimia nervosa is an illness where people eat large amounts of food in a short time (called bingeing) and then get rid of it either by vomiting or by taking laxatives (called purging). This may happen as little as twice a week or as often as twice a day over a period of months. It is hard to recognise people with bulimia because they appear to be of normal weight and the bingeing and purging take place in private. Bulimia is most common in women in their late teens and early 20s. But it can also occur in men and women of all ages. The body is affected by frequent vomiting or the taking of laxatives and may show these symptoms:

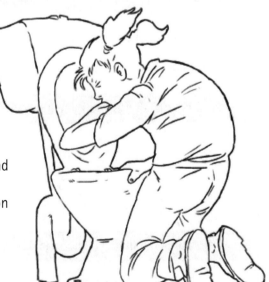

- severe tooth decay due to stomach acid attacking tooth enamel
- salivary glands swell up
- tears and bleeding in the oesophagus (pipe between mouth and stomach)
- constipation and bloating as bowel becomes dependent on laxatives
- irregular heartbeat due to lack of potassium
- very rarely the stomach can split because too much food is in it
- in women menstruation can be irregular.

Compulsive eating disorder also involves bingeing. But people with this disorder do not try to get rid of the food afterwards. Compulsive eating disorder is more common than anorexia and bulimia. It affects men more than the other eating disorders. It is often older people in their 30s and 40s who suffer from it.

If overeating causes people to become overweight or obese, they are at a greater risk of heart disease, high blood pressure and diabetes. It may involve the following:

- eating alone so no one sees how much you eat
- eating very quickly
- eating until uncomfortably full
- eating even when not hungry
- feeling upset about your eating behaviour.

Treating people with eating disorders often involves helping them to come to terms with the emotional and psychological problems that have lead to the problem. Firstly the person must want to change his or her eating habits. Then the person needs to seek specialist help. The more quickly someone receives treatment the more likely is complete recovery. Support from friends and family is important. If you have a problem with dieting, bingeing or weight loss, try to talk to a doctor or school nurse.

4U2DO

1 Give answers to the following.

a) What is believed to be the main cause of eating disorders? _____

b) Why do you think people suffering from anorexia feel weak, exhausted, faint and dizzy? _____

_____

c) What might be the long-term effect of not menstruating because of anorexia? _____

d) Why is it hard to identify people who are suffering from bulimia? _____

e) What behaviours might make you suspect that someone you know is suffering from bulimia? _____

_____

2 There are people in the community who can help if you or a friend is suffering from an eating disorder. Suggest where you could go for help to get back to healthy eating.

_____

_____

3 Find one thing in the unit that is associated with each of the following.

a) hormone imbalance _____ c) teenagers _____

b) loss of head hair _____ d) oesophagus _____

4 Write down 3 things you have learned from this unit.

a) _____

b) _____

c) _____

5 Write down anything you need to ask your teacher to explain.

_____

20

UNIT 09 CHILD OBESITY – ARE FAD DIETS THE ANSWER?

A recent report by The International Obesity Task Force said:

- at least 155 million children throughout the world, between the ages of 5 and 17 are too heavy. That is 10% of children in this age range.
- 45 million are considered to be obese and have an increased risk of developing diabetes, heart disease and other illnesses.
- there is a worldwide crisis in chronic diseases linked to bad eating habits and lack of exercise.

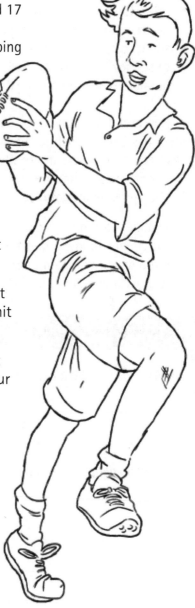

The Task Force wanted countries to develop national obesity action plans. It presented its findings to the World Health Organisation (WHO) where health ministers from around the world could consider a worldwide strategy on diet, physical activity and health.

In the fight against 'the bulge' many people try dieting. There are many diets available. Many feature in magazines and on television. Before you try the latest fad diets, you should know this information:

Extremely low-carbohydrate diets such as the Atkins diet, suggest you can eat all the meat, cheese, eggs and fat (like butter and oils) you like but you must limit your carbohydrates (to less than 100g per day).

The High Protein Low Carbohydrate Quick Weight Loss Diet™ removes what it calls refined carbohydrates (sugar, white rice, white bread and crackers) from your diet and replaces them with fibre-rich whole fruits, vegetables, brown rice and products made from whole wheat flour. It also encourages people to eat more protein foods.

Low carbohydrate diets are based on this idea:

1 Carbohydrates increase the blood sugar level. This stimulates the release of insulin that transfers the sugar from the blood to the cells to be used for energy. Excess sugars are stored as fats.

2 By restricting carbohydrates in the diet, less insulin is produced. The body uses stored fat for energy.

Dieticians and nutritionists have some concerns about diets that restrict the amount of carbohydrates so much. They suggest that:

- your body starts to use the protein and fat in your diet to get the glucose it needs for energy. This means they are not available for their proper use e.g. building muscle and repairing damaged tissue.
- your body may even begin to use (burn up) its own muscles and organs.
- you develop ketosis. This is having an abnormally high amount of substances called ketones in your blood due to excessive use of fats for energy. It causes very bad breath, abnormally high blood acid and may cause an irregular heart beat.
- a lot of the weight you lose at the start of the diet is water because glycogen (from carbohydrates) holds water. When you run down your glycogen stores, you lose water or dehydrate.
- once you go off the diet, you experience weight gain due to rehydration (your body stores water).

Extremely low-fat diets remove most or animal protein, and all fats, nuts and seeds from your diet. This may have short-term health benefits as people eat more fruit and vegetables and less processed food. But in the longer term it means:

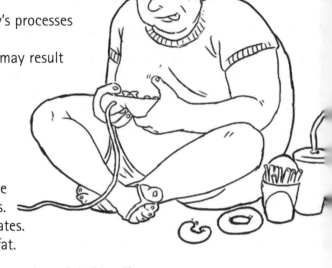

- the body lacks the building blocks to maintain the body's processes at a normal level.
- fat-soluble vitamins are not available to the body. This may result in irregular menstruation in women.
- some important minerals are lacking.
- raised levels of LDL or 'bad' cholesterol in the blood.
- possible reduced immunity to infections.

Research has shown that over the past 25 years where there has been a push for having less fat in your diet, there has been an increase in obesity, heart disease and diabetes. Frequently foods that are low in fat are high in carbohydrates. So they provide lots of glucose and the extra is stored as fat.

Fad diets are not successful in the long term. They can have harmful side effects. If you cannot follow a diet for the rest of your life, then it is not worthwhile. Eventually you will gain back the weight you have lost. The best approach to weight control is to combine a well-balanced diet with regular aerobic exercise.

4U2DO

1 Answer these questions.

a) What do you think has led to the high number of overweight and obese children in the world?

_____

_____

b) How do people who support low-carbohydrate diets believe the diet helps people to lose weight?

_____

_____

_____

_____

c) What is the best way to control your body weight and stay fit and healthy?

_____

_____

_____

2 Give 3 things you would want to see in New Zealand's national obesity plan

a) _____

b) _____

c) _____

3 Fill out the chart.

Low carbohydrate – high protein diets	
Advantages	Disadvantages

4 Give 3 ways low-fat diets may be harmful to the body.

a) _____

b) _____

c) _____

5 Put dashes (/) to show where each new word begins below.

rehydrationinsulinketosisobesityaerobicexercisedietsglycogendiabetes

6 Write down 3 things you have learned from this unit.

a) _____

b) _____

c) _____

7 Write down anything you need to ask your teacher to explain.

_____

_____

_____

UNIT 10 ELEMENTS, COMPOUNDS AND MIXTURES

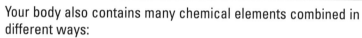

Sitting in your classroom at school or in your bedroom at home, you are surrounded by things made of a wide variety of materials e.g. wood, glass, metals, plastics, and fibres. These are all examples of matter. They are made from chemicals that are themselves made up of very small particles called atoms.

When a large number of atoms of one type are together, they become visible as a chemical element. There are 92 naturally occurring elements on Earth. Oxygen is the most plentiful. Oxygen makes up 20% of the air that we breathe. When it is combined with other elements it makes up:

- 89% of water
- 47% of the Earth's crust
- almost 50% of most rocks and minerals
- 65% of the human body.

Common elements that you come across in your everyday life include:

- chlorine (e.g. disinfects pools and drinking water)

- aluminium (e.g. drink cans and window frames)

- lead (e.g. sinkers)

- carbon (e.g. diamonds and pencil leads)

- red phosphorus (e.g. tip of matchsticks)

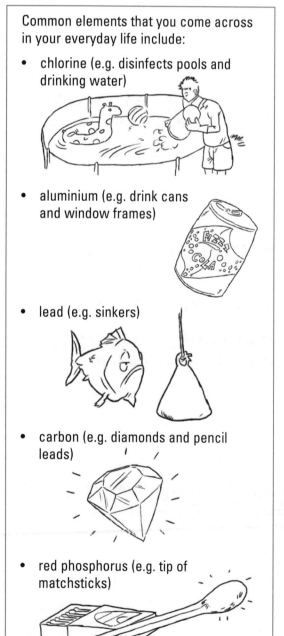

Your body also contains many chemical elements combined in different ways:

- the element oxygen – part of water and molecules that make up all living things
- the element carbon – part of organic molecules
- the element hydrogen – part of water and organic molecules
- the element nitrogen – part of proteins
- the element calcium – part of bones.

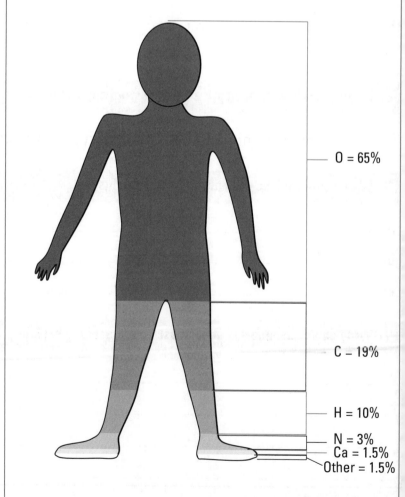

O = 65%

C – 19%

H = 10%

N = 3%
Ca = 1.5%
Other = 1.5%

- An element is made up of atoms, all of the same kind; so copper is made up just of copper atoms, gold is made up just of gold atoms.
- An element cannot be broken down into simpler substances.
- An element cannot be made by combining simpler substances.

GOLD AS AN EXAMPLE OF AN ELEMENT

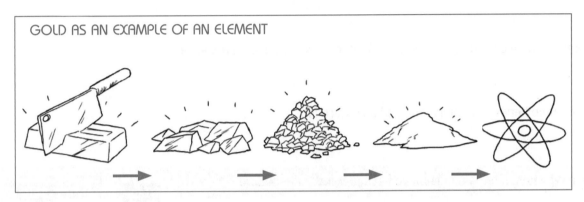

Atoms combine chemically to form compounds, which have different properties from the atoms they are made from. Water is a compound made when 2 hydrogen atoms combine with 1 oxygen atom. Hydrogen and oxygen are both gases at room temperature and normal atmospheric pressure; water is a liquid.

Sodium chloride or table salt is a white crystal you sprinkle on the food you eat. But it is made from atoms of chlorine (a poisonous, greenish-yellow gas) and sodium (a highly reactive, soft, grey metal stored in oil).

Just as compounds can be made by chemically combining atoms, it is possible to break them down, by chemical means, into the elements of which they are made.

Water can be broken up into hydrogen and oxygen gases by a process called electrolysis. An electric current is passed through water via two electrodes connected to a power supply. Bubbles of hydrogen form at one electrode and oxygen forms at the other electrode.

Electrolysis of water

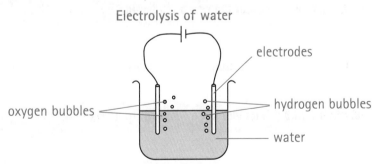

electrodes

oxygen bubbles

hydrogen bubbles

water

A mixture is where two or more separate substances are mixed physically together. But they are not chemically combined. The substances that make up the mixture keep their own properties. The salt water that covers two thirds of the Earth's surface is a mixture. It is made up of water with salt (sodium chloride) and other mineral salts dissolved in it. Even though you cannot see the salt in the water, you can taste it.

Mixtures can be separated into their components by physical processes such as filtering, distilling, chromatography and using magnets.

4U2DO

1 Name 3 chemical elements present in your classroom.

a) _____ b) _____ c) _____

2 Finish these sentences.

a) If you could break up an aluminium can into the smallest particle it is made of, that particle would be

_____

b) Table salt (sodium chloride) is a compound rather than an element because _____

_____

c) The difference between a compound and a mixture is _____

_____

3 Explain why tap water is a compound but salt water is a mixture.

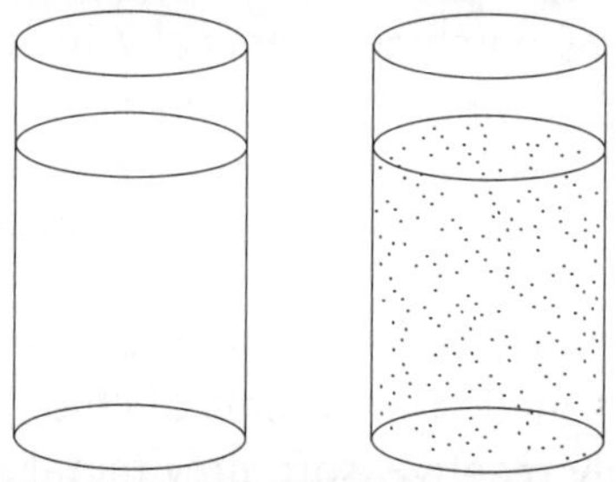

_____

_____

_____

_____

Tap   Salt

4 Complete, by labels and colours, the following table to show what proportion of oxgyen each has.

water	
Earth's crust	
most rocks and minerals	
human body	

0%   100%

5 In the list below colour the compounds red, the mixtures blue and the elements yellow.

chlorine	hydrogen	oxygen	salty water	sodium chloride	water

6 Write down 3 things you have learned from this unit.

a) _____

b) _____

c) _____

7 Write down anything you need to ask your teacher to explain.

_____

26

PHOTOCOPYING PROHIBITED

UNIT

11 SEPARATING MIXTURES

M E T H O D S

S E P A R A T I N G

When two or more substances are physically combined, a mixture is formed. Sometimes it is easy to see the parts of the mixture e.g. grains of rice in a pot of water. Other times it is not possible to see the different parts that make the mixture e.g. salt dissolved in water.

Because the substances are only physically combined, they can be separated using physical separating techniques. Some, such as pouring cooked rice through a sieve so the water is removed, you use at home. Other methods, such as distillation, are carried out in science labs or places like oil refineries.

FILTERING

= one of the simplest methods used to separate solid particles from the liquid part of a mixture.

A sieve or colander separates cooked food from the water in which the food has been boiled.

A teabag stops tea leaves getting into the water in a cup.

In a science lab the mixture is poured through filter paper. This paper has very small holes in it. The holes let liquid through but not the solid part of the mixture.

EVAPORATION / CRYSTALLISATION

= can be used to separate a dissolved solid from a liquid e.g. salt from seawater. The mixture is heated so the water turns into water vapour leaving the salt crystals behind.

At Lake Grassmere near Blenheim, water slowly evaporates from seawater stored in shallow holding basins and the salt is collected for processing into table salt.

Rain puddles evaporate in the sun. They leave behind small particles of dirt and dust collected as the rain fell through the atmosphere.

In a science lab the mixture is put in an evaporating basin and heated with a Bunsen burner to remove the liquid part.

CHROMATOGRAPHY

= used to separate mixtures of coloured substances e.g. the inks combined to produce the black ink in a felt pen or the different pigments contained in a leaf. Different sized chemical pigments move at different rates through the paper. A special type of chromatography called gel electrophoresis is used in DNA fingerprinting. Smaller fragments move further through the gel than larger fragments. The result is something that looks like a bar code.

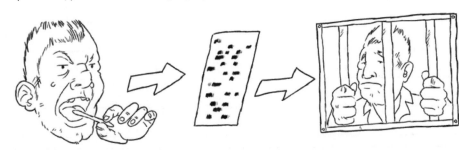

SEPARATING METHODS

DISTILLATION

= used to separate mixtures of liquids by using our knowledge of boiling points and changes of state. The liquid mixture is boiled and the vapours collected and condensed.

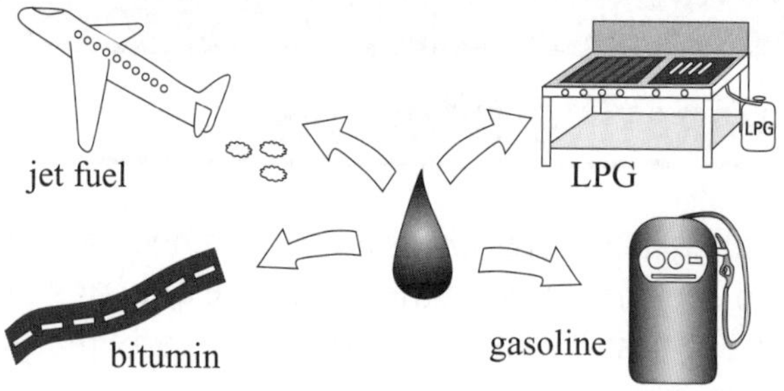

jet fuel
LPG
LPG
bitumin
gasoline

This process is used at the Marsden Point Oil Refinery near Whangarei where crude oil (petroleum) is separated into many different products.

CENTRIFUGING

= separates substances of different densities by spinning tubes containing the mixture very rapidly in a horizontal circle.

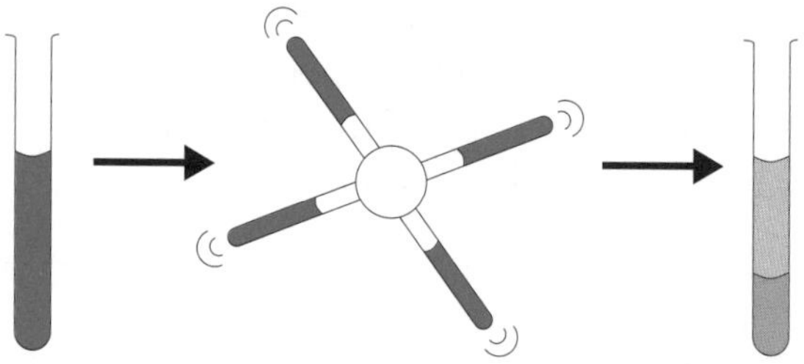

The mixtures are usually a solid in a liquid such as the blood cells in blood plasma or the cream in whole milk.

MAGNETISM

= used to separate a mixture that contains iron or steel because these metals are attracted to a magnet while other substances are not.

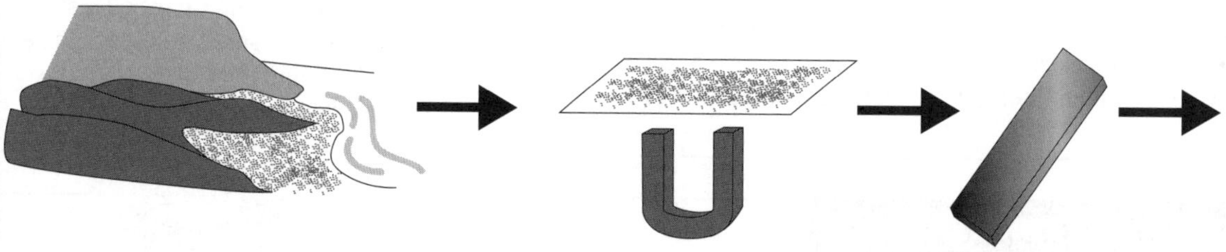

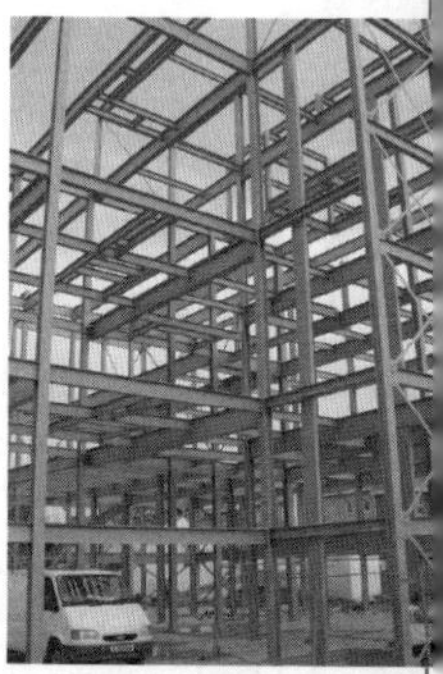

On the west coast of the North Island near the Waikato Heads black sand containing the iron mineral magnetite is mined. The sand is trucked to a plant near the coast where magnets are used to separate the magnetite from the sand and other non-magnetic material. In the last stage at this plant, water is added to the ironsand concentrate so that it can be pumped through pipelines to the Glenbrook steel mill south of Auckland where it is used in the smelting of iron, which is then used to make steel. The non-magnetic sands that are not required are returned to the mining area.

4U2DO

1 Circle the mixtures in the list below.

- nuts and bolts
- human blood
- a cup of sugared coffee
- ironsand
- pen ink
- crude oil
- water
- hydrochloric acid

2 Fill out the chart.

Separation method	What it is used to separate

3 Separating methods.

a) Number, in the order you would carry out the separations, the equipment you would use to separate a mixture of iron filings, sugar and rice grains all together in a glass of water.

( )	( )	( )
filter funnel	evaporating basin	chromatography paper
( )	( )	( )
centrifuge	Leibig Condenser	magnet

b) List or draw the equipment you would use to separate salt from seawater.

4 Check out the diagram and give answers to the questions.

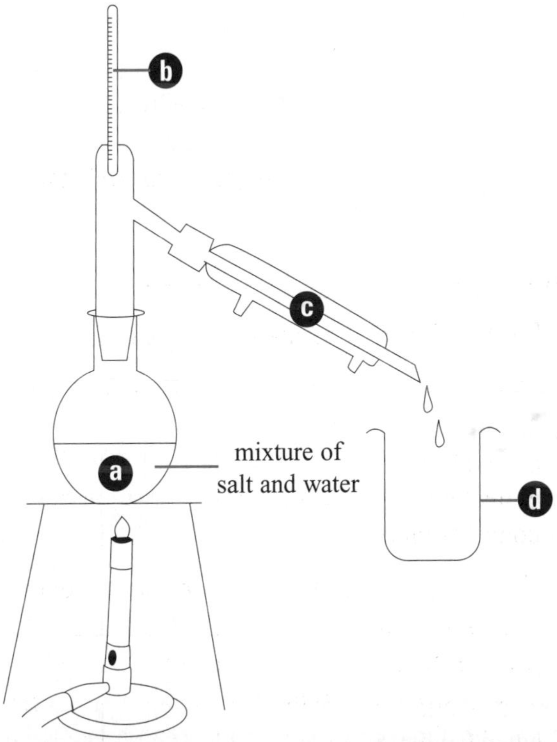

a) What is happening to the mixture at **a**?

_____

_____

b) What will the reading be on **b**?

_____

c) What is happening at **c**?

_____

_____

d) What will be collected at **d**?

_____

mixture of salt and water

5 Write down 3 things you have learned from this unit.

a) _____

b) _____

c) _____

6 Write down anything you need to ask your teacher to explain.

_____

UNIT 12 ATOMS, ELEMENTS AND THE PERIODIC TABLE

Atoms are the building blocks of chemical elements. Each element, such as chlorine, oxygen and lead, is made up of only one type of atom. Atoms themselves are made up of 3 smaller sub-atomic particles called **protons**, **neutrons** and **electrons**.

- The protons and neutrons are found in the centre of the atom called the nucleus. They are the heavy part of an atom.

- Electrons move very rapidly around the nucleus in areas called shells or clouds. They are much lighter than protons and neutrons but take up a lot of space. They take part in chemical reactions to form new compounds.

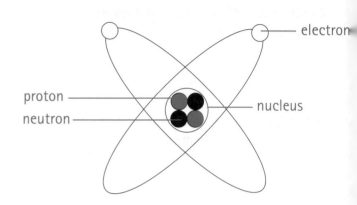

In some ways an atom is like our solar system. The nucleus is the sun and the electrons are the planets that orbit the sun.

The **Periodic Table of Elements** lists all the known elements, both naturally occurring and man-made, in a special way. Here is part of the Periodic Table:

The elements are listed in columns (called **groups**). The members of each group belong to a chemical family. In chemical reactions they behave in similar ways. Those in Group 1 are very reactive while those in Group 18 are unreactive.

The elements are listed in rows (or **periods**) and as you move from left to right the number of protons (the Atomic Number) in the nucleus increases, e.g. Carbon (C) has 6 protons, Nitrogen (N) has 7 and Oxygen (O) has 8.

Period	Group 1	Group 2		Group 13	Group 14	Group 15	Group 16	Group 17	Group 18
Period 1	1 **H** Hydrogen								2 **He** Helium
Period 2	3 **Li** Lithium	4 **Be** Beryllium		5 **B** Boron	6 **C** Carbon	7 **N** Nitrogen	8 **O** Oxygen	9 **F** Flourine	10 **Ne** Neon
Period 3	11 **Na** Sodium	12 **Mg** Magnesium		13 **Al** Aluminium	14 **Si** Silicon	15 **P** Phosphorus	16 **S** Sulfur	17 **Cl** Chlorine	18 **Ar** Argon
Period 4	19 **K** Potassium	20 **Ca** Calcium							

Each element is represented by a chemical symbol of one or two letters. Usually it is the first letter or first two letters of their name, e.g. O = oxygen, C = carbon, Ca = calcium. Some elements have symbols that refer to their name in the Latin language, e.g. Fe = iron (Latin name was ferrum) Cu = copper (Latin name was cuprum) Pb = lead (Latin name was plumbum).

The elements that are metals are found on the left hand side and middle of the table while the non-metals are found on the right hand side. The exception is hydrogen, which is a non-metal, not a metal. It is on the left and in group 1 because it behaves like a metal in a chemical reaction.

1 Give names for the following.

a) 2 metal elements that you use in your everyday life _____

b) 1 gaseous element present in the air you breathe _____

c) the metal element that is unusual because it is a liquid at room temperature _____

d) an element that, when dissolved in ethanol, is used as an antiseptic _____

2 Name the element shown.

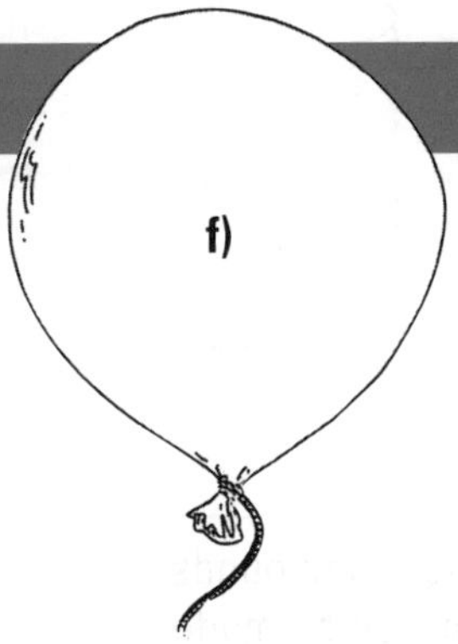

a) _____ b) _____ c) _____

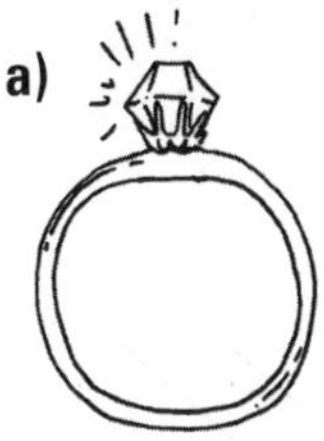

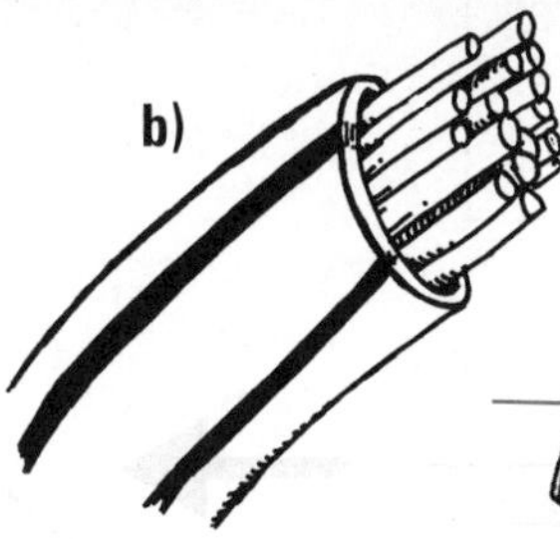

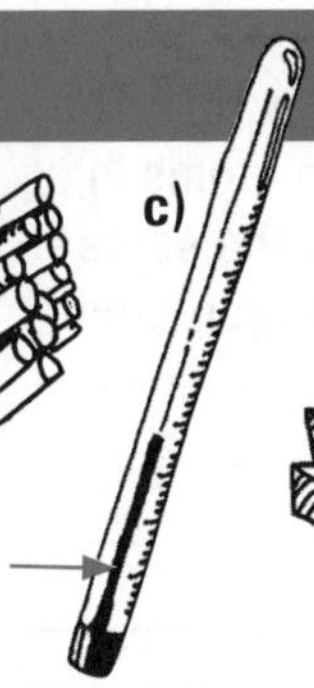

d) _____ e) _____ f) _____

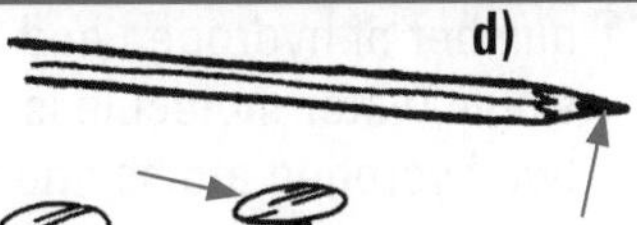

3 Draw a diagram to show the solar system model of an atom. Label the nucleus and show where the protons, neutrons and electrons are found.

4 Write the name of the element next to the chemical symbols.

a) O _____ b) C _____ c) He _____ d) F _____

5 Give the correct chemical symbol for the following.

a) hydrogen _____ b) chlorine _____ c) iron _____ d) lead _____

6 Write down 3 things you have learned from this unit.

a) _____

b) _____

c) _____

7 Write down anything you need to ask your teacher to explain.

_____

UNIT 13 COMPOUNDS

A compound is made when different elements chemically join together.

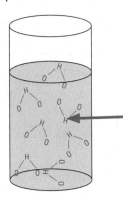

Water is a compound made up from the elements hydrogen and oxygen.

The chemical formula for water is H_2O. The number of hydrogen and oxygen atoms in a single water molecule is always the same – two hydrogen atoms and one oxygen atom.

Other compounds can also be made from hydrogen and oxygen atoms. But the proportions of each atom are different so the compound has different physical and chemical properties.

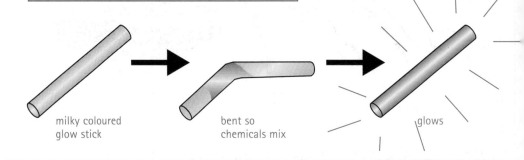

milky coloured glow stick

bent so chemicals mix

glows

Combining the elements hydrogen and oxygen also makes hydrogen peroxide. But it has the chemical formula H_2O_2. This tells you that there are two hydrogen and two oxygen atoms joined together. Hydrogen peroxide can be used as a mild antiseptic to treat wounds, a bleaching agent for cloth and hair, and it is one of the chemicals used in the reaction inside a glow stick when you snap the stick to produce the glow.

Elements chemically combine during a chemical reaction. These reactions involve some of the electrons that are moving around the nucleus of an atom. When elements react together:

- atoms of one element may lose some of their electrons to atoms of another element
- atoms of one element may gain electrons from atoms of another element
- atoms of one element may share their electrons with atoms of another element.

Atoms gain, lose or share electrons to become chemically stable. The atoms are then chemically bonded to each other. Once atoms from different elements join together in this way they form a new substance, a compound, which has different properties from the elements that it is made from.

Chemical reactions do not only take place in test tubes in science laboratories. One chemical reaction you will have seen happening in many places around you everyday is rusting.

Rust looks very different to the iron, oxygen and water that are needed to make it and it behaves differently too. It is believed that early people used ground iron oxide to make a red paint that they used to paint pictures on cave walls.

Rust, that reddish brown, flaky crust that forms on many things made from iron or steel, is a compound called hydrated iron oxide ($Fe_2O_3.H_2O$). For rusting to occur, both water and oxygen must be present.

In this reaction iron atoms give some electrons to the oxygen atoms that are dissolved in water.

PREVENTING RUST

Rust can be prevented in many ways but they all work by preventing the metal coming in contact with oxygen and water. Examples: paint, plastic coating, oil, galvanising.

 nail +   water +   oxygen =   rust

1 Circle the chemical formulas that show compounds in the list below.

O_2 CO_2 H_2O_2 H_2 H_2O

2 The formula for a glucose molecule is $C_6H_{12}O_6$. Give the following.

a) the names of the 3 elements that make up this molecule _____

b) how many atoms of each element there are _____

3 Answer the following.

a) What is the difference between a compound and a mixture? _____

_____

b) Which part of an atom is involved in a chemical reaction? _____

4 In the spaces provided describe each of the substances that react together to form rust, and also describe rust.

Iron	Water	Oxygen	Rust

5 Look at the diagrams of things made from iron. Write down how each one is treated to stop it rusting.

 a)	 b)	 c)	 d)

6 Write down 3 things you have learned from this unit.

a) _____

b) _____

c) _____

7 Write down anything you need to ask your teacher to explain.

_____

UNIT 14 OXYGEN – THE ELEMENT OF LIFE

Oxygen is a colourless, odourless gas. Either by itself or combined with other elements, it makes up about 20% of our atmosphere, 47% of the Earth's crust and 65% of our bodies.

Oxygen is the 8th element on the periodic table. This means it has 8 protons in its nucleus and 8 electrons moving around the nucleus.

Oxygen occurs in the air we breathe as a diatomic molecule (O_2). This means there are 2 oxygen atoms joined together.

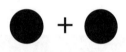

2 oxygen atoms   oxygen molecule

Oxygen is produced by plants as a product of photosynthesis. In the leaves of plants, water and carbon dioxide combine using the energy of sunlight to produce glucose and oxygen. This oxygen diffuses out of the leaves through the stomata (tiny pores) on the underside of the leaf and into the atmosphere.

Almost all living things use oxygen in their bodies to produce the energy they need to grow, repair cells, reproduce and carry out all other life processes. In humans the oxygen in the air breathed into the lungs passes through the walls of the lungs into the bloodstream where it attaches to the red blood cells that carry it to all the body's cells. In the process of respiration, the oxygen is used to break down sugars in the cells to release energy. Carbon dioxide is produced during respiration. It is carried back to the lungs in the blood plasma. It passes into the lungs and is breathed out.

Oxygen is necessary for combustion (burning) to take place. A fuel of some kind is also needed, as oxygen itself will not burn. Most fuels contain the element carbon. When things burn, the carbon they contain combines with oxygen to produce carbon dioxide. Heat and light are given off in the reaction. A fire burns hotter in pure oxygen than in air that is only 20% oxygen. To stop fires, the fuel needs to be deprived of oxygen. This can be as simple as covering the fire with a wet blanket or some other non-flammable cover.

Oxyacetylene torches are used to cut or weld metals. By adding oxygen to acetylene gas, a flame with a temperature of over 3000°C can be produced. To weld metals, the torch is used to melt the edges of the metals before they are fused together. In cutting metals, the torch is used to heat the metal but not melt it. Oxygen is sprayed in a fine line across the hot metal. It burns through to leave a cut edge.

Ozone Hole

15–50 km above the Earth's surface is a layer called the ozone layer. Ozone is trioxygen (O_3). It protects living things on Earth by absorbing harmful ultraviolet (UV) radiation from the sun. Ozone is formed in the upper atmosphere when UV radiation splits O_2 molecules into oxygen atoms. These loose atoms then join on to oxygen molecules to form O_3. Ozone is formed in the same way in the lower atmosphere when lightning breaks up oxygen molecules. This ozone quickly turns back into regular oxygen. Chloroflourocarbons (CFCs) were used in aerosol cans as a propellant until it was discovered that they were responsible for destroying ozone. Now their use is banned in many countries. A 'hole' in the ozone layer over Antarctica allows more ultraviolet light through which in turn leads to more skin cancer.

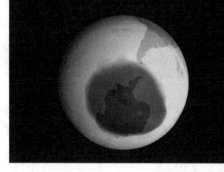

1   Fill out the oxygen profile.

OXYGEN

Symbol _____	State _____
Smell _____	Colour _____
Position on Periodic Table _____	Produced by plants _____
Uses for living things _____	Required for combustion Yes/No
Why added to acetylene gas _____	Place (function) in ozone _____

2   Give answers to these questions.

a) Why is oxygen the element of life? _____

b) Where does the oxygen in the air we breathe, come from? _____

c) Why should people living in New Zealand be concerned about the 'hole' in the ozone layer?

_____

d) How does ozone in the atmosphere help us? _____

e) What does CFC stand for? _____

3   Show how each of the following numbers are connected to oxygen.

a) 8 _____

b) 2 _____

c) 15–20 _____

d) 3000 _____

4   Check out the drawing and write down what the person should have done.

The person should have _____

_____

_____

5   Write down 3 things you have learned from this unit.

a) _____

b) _____

c) _____

6   Write down anything you need to ask your teacher to explain.

_____

UNIT 15 HYDROGEN – AN EXPLOSIVE ELEMENT

Hydrogen:

- is the most plentiful element in the universe
- is part of water
- is a large part of the sun and many stars
- is present in most acids and plastics
- has an atomic number of 1
- is the lightest known element
- is part of all the organic molecules that make up plant and animal tissue
- joins with carbon to form hydrocarbons that include petroleum and natural gas.

Hydrogen gas was used in early airships. In World War 1 the airships were used as bombers and to protect ships from submarine attack. In the 1930s they were popular as passenger ships. The Hindenberg, built in 1936, was the largest airship (245m long and 41m wide). It had a cruising speed of 125 kilometres per hour. It carried passengers across the Atlantic. On May 6, 1937 the Hindenberg exploded as it was coming in to dock in New Jersey killing 35 people on board and one person on the ground. Today, small airships called blimps are used for advertising. They contain helium, which is the second lightest element. Helium is unreactive so will not catch fire.

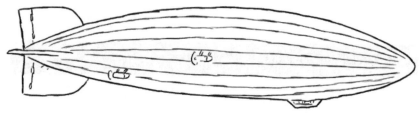

Hydrogen could be the fuel of the future. A fuel cell is a device that converts hydrogen and oxygen into water producing electricity and heat in the process. A single Proton Exchange Membrane (PEM) fuel cell can produce only 0.7 volts of electrical energy but the cells can be combined in a cell stack to produce more energy. The motor industry is developing cars that use several cell stacks. The car carries a hydrogen supply but uses oxygen from the air. The only emission from the car is water vapour so it is good for the environment. Using hydrogen could prevent our fossil fuels such as oil, natural gas and coal from running out. Hydrogen does not produce carbon dioxide which is contributing to global warming.

Hydrogen is also an important ingredient in the manufacturing of ammonia. Ammonia is a part of many fertilisers such as ammonium phosphate, ammonium nitrate and urea. Farmers apply these fertilisers to pastures to add nitrogen to the soil. When absorbed by grass and other plants, nitrogen is used to build proteins and they are used to make new plant tissue. Animals eating plants can then use plant protein to build up their own tissues.

Fill it up with gas. No, not petrol, H gas.

---

1   Tick the items that contain hydrogen.

☐ petroleum	☐ plant tissue	☐ ammonia	☐ Hindendberg
☐ the universe	☐ animal tissue	☐ water	☐ helium
☐ the sun	☐ hydrocarbons	☐ natural gas	

2 Tick which one you would rather travel in, and say why.

HYDROGEN

HELIUM

Why: _____

3 Put the following in the best order to show start to finish.

grass uses nitrogen to build proteins and new plant tissue **(A)**	hydrogen helps make ammonia **(B)**	animals use plant protein to build up own tissues **(C)**
fertiliser absorbed by grass and other plants **(D)**	ammonia helps make fertiliser such as ammonium phosphate **(E)**	farmers apply fertiliser to pastures to add nitrogen **(F)**
		animals eat grass **(G)**

order: _____

4 Think of answers for these questions.

a) What makes hydrogen the lightest element known? _____

b) Why is helium used in birthday balloons? _____

c) Why is the use of hydrogen to make fertilisers important for New Zealand? _____

_____

5 Put comments in the speech bubbles that you would use to explain to someone why using hydrogen to power cars is better than using fossil fuels such as oil and petrol.

6 Write down 3 things you have learned from this unit.

a) _____

b) _____

c) _____

7 Write down anything you need to ask your teacher to explain.

_____

UNIT 16 CARBON DIOXIDE – FIZZ AND FOAM

Carbon dioxide:

- is colourless
- is odourless
- is a gas
- makes up only 0.04% of our atmosphere and yet is vital to life on Earth.

Carbon dioxide is used by plants in the process of photosynthesis. This produces glucose, that plants use to provide the energy they need to live and oxygen, which most living things need to survive. Carbon dioxide is produced in the cells of living things as a result of respiration. This is the process that gives living things the energy they need to power life's processes.

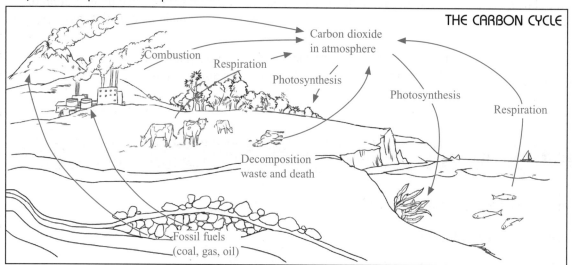

THE CARBON CYCLE

Carbon dioxide in atmosphere

Combustion

Respiration

Photosynthesis

Photosynthesis

Respiration

Decomposition waste and death

Fossil fuels (coal, gas, oil)

Carbon dioxide has many other uses in our everyday lives.

- Some fire extinguishers contain carbon dioxide gas that is pressurised to form a liquid. When the pressure is released by squeezing the trigger, the liquid is released and becomes a gas that smothers a fire. This is because carbon dioxide is heavier than air and does not support combustion. This type of extinguisher is good for what are called class C fires involving motors and electrical equipment.

- The fizz in soft drinks is due to the presence of carbon dioxide. The carbon dioxide is dissolved under pressure. When you open the top of a drink can, you release the pressure. The carbon dioxide bubbles rise to the surface. Some homes have a 'sodastream' machine so people can make their own soft drinks. A cylinder of carbon dioxide in the machine forces the gas into a bottle of water; flavoured syrup is added to make the drink.

- Yeasts are one-celled organisms that are used in bread-making. They use sugar added to the flour, or the glucose from the breakdown of flour, in the process of respiration. This provides the energy the yeasts need to grow. Carbon dioxide is produced as a waste product in this process and this makes the bread dough rise. In the oven the heat causes the bubbles of gas to expand and the bread rises more as it cooks. The heat of the oven also kills the yeasts.

- At -78.5°C, carbon dioxide turns into a solid called dry ice. As it warms, dry ice turns straight into a gas rather than melting into a liquid. Dry ice is used to refrigerate food, medicine and other things that would be damaged if ice made from water were used.

Carbon dioxide is having a major impact on the Earth's environment.

Burning fossil fuels such as coal, oil, petrol and natural gas releases carbon dioxide into the atmosphere. Carbon dioxide levels in the atmosphere have increased 12% in the last 100 years.

Over the past 100 years Earth's average temperature has risen by 0.5°C. This may not seem much but global warming can change rainfall and weather patterns. That will affect plant and animal populations, and agriculture and horticulture. It may melt polar caps, giving a rise in sea level.

Cutting down large areas of rainforest means fewer trees to use the carbon dioxide in photosynthesis. This increase in carbon dioxide is the main contributor to global warming. The Earth absorbs ultraviolet radiation from the Sun and reradiates infrared radiation. This is then absorbed by carbon dioxide and other gases to blanket Earth in warm air. This is called the greenhouse effect.

Countries have made an agreement called the Kyoto Protocol. It aims to limit global warming. It wants to reduce the amount of greenhouse gases such as carbon dioxide released into the air.

1 Fill out the profile on carbon dioxide.

Symbol _____

Colour _____

% of atmosphere _____

Lighter or heavier than air _____

Change at −78.5°C _____

State _____

Smell _____

Combustibility _____

Use by plants _____

Impact on environment _____

2 Is carbon dioxide an element or a compound? Explain your answer.

_____

_____

3 Explain how the element carbon is recycled through living things.

_____

_____

4 Write labels and short notes on the drawing to help explain how it works.

5 Suggest answers to these questions.

a) Why is carbon dioxide used in fire extinguishers? _____

_____

b) Why do soft drinks go 'flat' when they have been left open for a while? _____

_____

c) Why do bakers use yeast when they make bread? _____

_____

d) What are the advantages of using dry ice rather than ordinary ice to refrigerate food and medicine?

_____

e) Why is it important that countries sign the Kyoto Protocol? _____

_____

6 Write down how the event in each picture contributes to global warming/the greenhouse effect.

 a)	 b)	 c)	 d)

7 Write down 3 things you have learned from this unit.

a) _____

b) _____

c) _____

8 Write down anything you need to ask your teacher to explain.

_____

UNIT 17 PLASTICS — THE MATERIAL OF OUR TIME

- Plastics are materials that can be shaped into any shape or form by applying heat or pressure.

- The name plastic comes from the Greek word 'plastikos' meaning 'to be shaped'.

- Plastics have replaced more traditional materials such as wood, metal, glass, ceramics and fibres in our everyday lives.

- Plastics are being used more and more because they are stronger, lighter, longer lasting and require less maintenance than traditional materials. Plastics are often less expensive to make and they can be made to do a job no other material can be used for.

Plastics are an excellent example of how elements can combine in countless ways to form a wide variety of new compounds.

Many things which were once made of paper, glass, wood or metal are now made of plastic.

Polystyrene and polythene are made from the elements carbon and hydrogen joined together to form long chains or **polymers** (poly means many). Each polymer is made up of thousands of smaller molecules called **monomers** (mono means one). In polystyrene many styrene molecules are joined together and in polythene many ethene molecules are joined together. If air is blown through polystyrene plastic while it is hot it makes foam rather than a flat plastic.

Both polystyrene and polythene are examples of thermoplastics. This means they can be repeatedly softened by heating and hardened by cooling which allows them to be recycled.

Polystyrene products | Polythene products

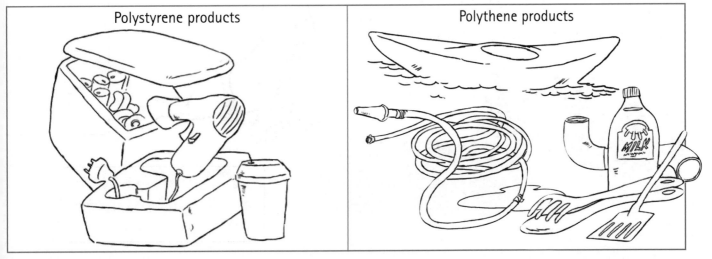

Another group of plastics are called **thermosetting plastics**. They are soft to start with but change irreversibly to a hard rigid form so they cannot be reshaped and reused. They include:

- **Epoxy** – water and weather resistant plastic, hardens quickly, has high bond strength, used in adhesives and protective coatings.

- **Polyurethane** – tough and resistant to chemicals, used in electrical insulation, paints and varnishes.

- **Silicone** – resists weather, has high elasticity, has good electrical qualities, used for electrical fittings, lubricants and waterproof materials.

Epoxy	Polyurethane	Silicone
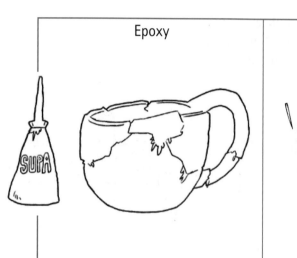		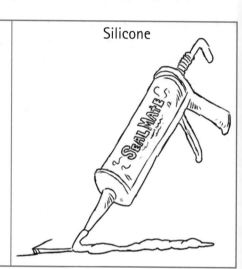

A problem with plastics is that they take a long time to decompose or break down once they have been thrown away. Objects made from thermoplastics can be melted down and made into new plastic products but thermosetting plastics cannot. Thermosets are ground into powders or shredded. Shredded plastic is used as fillers in things like quilted jackets and sleeping bags. Many places recycle plastics but this does not happen everywhere.

Traditional plastics are made from non-renewable resources such as oil, coal and natural gas. Now available are biodegradable plastics made from natural plant polymers such as starch. These plastics can be broken down by micro-organisms so are better for the environment. Unfortunately they cost more than traditional plastics so are not as popular.

Polylactide (PLA) is a biodegradable plastic made from starch. The monomers used to make it are lactic acid. It is used to make plant pots and disposable nappies. Because it can be broken down in the body, it has biomedical uses.

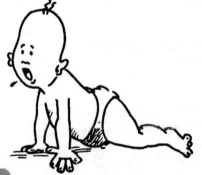

ANSWERS (this 4-page section is removable)

Unit 1   FOOD

1 a) individual e.g. guinea pig, rabbit, horse; b) carnivores e.g. dog, cat; c) omnivore e.g. chimpanzee, pet dog or cat; d) individual e.g. milk, butter, cheese; e) carbohydrates, proteins, fats, vitamins and minerals

2 kina = algae on rock; herbivore = leaf, nuts; vegetarian = butter, eggs, cheese, nuts; cockroach = ham, butter, eggs, cheese, nuts; omnivore = ham, butter, leaf, eggs, cheese, nuts; vegan = leaf, nuts

3 energy/heal quickly/normal body temperature/healthy

4 vegetarians = dairy products; vegans = nuts/lentils

Unit 2   CARBOHYDRATES

1 a) individual – should relate to need for energy; b) pasta is a complex carbohydrate so it will slowly release its energy and that is important for a marathon runner; c) fruit and vegetables provide fibre in our diets keeping our digestive system healthy, contain vitamins and minerals and also carbohydrates for energy

2 a) complex, b) simple, c) complex, d) simple, e) complex, f) complex

3 Glycogen stores excess glucose in liver and muscles

4 a) individual e.g. soft drinks, sweets, cakes, biscuits; b) individual – starchy foods e.g. bread, potato, pasta, rice

5 individual e.g. bananas, dates, kiwifruit, pineapple

6 a) dates have a high GI so provide energy quickly, b) spaghetti has a low GI so provides energy slowly

Unit 3   PROTEIN

1 haemoglobin carries oxygen, antibodies fight disease, hormones carry messages, enzymes control cell reactions, build cells and tissue

2 individual e.g. meat, cheese, milk, butter

3 a) children's bodies are growing so they need protein to make new cells and tissues; b) New Zealand farms produce a lot of protein foods so it is relatively cheap and easy to buy; c) breast milk supplies all nutritional needs of children; d) individual e.g. send surplus dairy food/milk biscuits/medical aid

4 11 – non essential amino acids / 9 – essential amino acids

Unit 4   FATS

1 a) individual e.g. butter, cheese, whole milk, meat; b) fats are used mainly for energy but also for warmth (insulation), to make hormones, for healthy hair and skin, to store Vitamins A, D, K, E; c) you should eat unsaturated fats such as plant oils; d) olive oil, corn oil, avocado oil

2 a) twice, b) fatty foods, c) unsaturated fats, d) insulate/make hormones/healthy skin and hair/store vitamins/keep body temperature

3 a) saturated, b) fat, c) obesity, d) unsaturated, e) fats

Unit 5   ENERGY VALUES OF FOOD

1 a) a food's energy b) 1000 c) stores it

2 a) bacon, b) because it provides more energy than cornflakes

3 labels from left to right = over 30/25–30/20–25/less than 20 = underweight/desirable/overweight/obese

4 a) individual BMI calculation, b) individual evaluation of body size

5 a) days when you do more exercise to provide enough energy; b) days when you do less exercise because you need less energy

6 a) individual list of food eaten in a day, b) individual value judgement on type of food eaten, c) individual based on food eaten, d) individual based on food not eaten

Unit 6   VITAMINS AND MINERALS, WATER AND FIBRE

1 a) silver beet; b) carrot; c) orange, d) peanuts, whole grains, egg yolk; e) individual e.g. orange, lemon, mandarin, grapefruit; f) Vitamin D is made in the skin when it is exposed to sunlight

2 a) milk; b) there is a lack of oxygen in the blood; c) girls lose blood when they menstruate; d) water is used for many things in the body e.g. in blood, to remove wastes, for chemical reactions; e) cereals are made from plant material so they contain cellulose that we cannot digest

3 a) to provide them with fibre to keep their digestive systems healthy; b) you need only small amounts of vitamins and any vitamins your body does not used is passed out in urine; c) lime juice contains vitamin C and prevents scurvy

4 a) goitre – sea food; b) anaemia – red meat, egg, leafy greens; c) rickets – dairy products; d) scurvy – citrus fruits, broccoli

Unit 7   DIGESTION AND THE DIGESTIVE SYSTEM

1 labels as on page 16

2 a) food is chewed by teeth; b) saliva contains enzymes; c) vomit contains stomach acid; d) a mix of simple chemicals in water, looks like soup; e) pass solid waste (faeces) regularly

3 a) take food in; b) break food down; c) take food chemicals into blood; d) pass undigested food out of body; e) indigestible food; f) where earthworms grind their food; g) tube to carry food to stomach; h) first part of small intestine; i) folds in wall of small intestine; j) large intestine; k) poo; l) speed up reactions

4 individual e.g. the enzymes break down the food stain into simple chemicals that can be dissolved in the soap powder

Unit 8   EATING DISORDERS

1 a) emotional or psychological problems; b) not enough food to supply the body with energy; c) can not have children later in life; d) they appear to be normal weight, purging takes place in private; e) individual e.g. going to the toilet straight after eating, eating big meals but not putting on weight

2 school nurse, family doctor, guidance counsellor

3 a) individual e.g. eating disorders; b) individual e.g. anorexia; c) individual e.g. at risk from anorexia; d) individual e.g. damaged in people with bulimia

Unit 9   CHILD OBESITY – ARE FAD DIETS THE ANSWER?

1 a) lack of exercise, increased amount of food eaten in a day, more fatty and sugary foods eaten, more processed (fast) food eaten; b) make the body produce less insulin so the body uses stored fat for energy; c) combine a well-balanced diet with regular aerobic exercise

2 individual e.g. compulsory PE in schools at all levels, control food sold in school canteens, reduce sales of fast foods

3 advantages = people eat more fibre foods including fruit and vegetables; disadvantages = may develop ketosis, body may break down own muscle to provide energy

4 the body lacks the building blocks to maintain the body's processes at a normal level, fat-soluble vitamins are not available to the body; this may result in irregular menstruation

in women, some important minerals are lacking, raised levels of LDL or 'bad' cholesterol in the blood, possible reduced immunity to infections

5 rehydration/insulin/ketosis/obesity/aerobic/exercise/diets/glycogen/diabetes

TOPIC 2 EVERYDAY ELEMENTS AND COMPOUNDS

Unit 10 ELEMENTS, COMPOUNDS AND MIXTURES
1 individual e.g. oxygen, iron, and aluminium

2 a) an aluminium atom; b) because it is made up of 2 different elements that have been chemically combined; c) in a compound the components are chemically combined but in a mixture the components are only physically combined

3 in the salt water the salt can be separated from the water by evaporating off the water; tap water contains the compound H_2O and is not a physical mixture so cannot be separated by simple techniques such as evaporation

4 water 89%; Earth's crust 47%; rocks and minerals 50%; human body 65%

5 compounds = sodium chloride and water; mixtures = salty water; elements = chlorine, hydrogen, oxygen

Unit 11 SEPARATING MIXTURES
1 the mixtures are nuts and bolts, crude oil, cup of sugared coffee, human blood, iron sand, pen ink

2

Separation method	What it is used to separate
filtering	a solid from a liquid
evaporation	a dissolved solid from a liquid
chromotography	mixtures of coloured substances
distillation	liquids with different boiling points
centrifusion	substances of different densities
magnetism	magnetic substances from non-magnetic materials

3 a) 1st = magnet, 2nd = filter funnel, 3rd = either condenser or evaporating basin; b) individual

4 a) boiling; b) 100°C; c) water condensing; d) water

Unit 12 ATOMS, ELEMENTS AND THE PERIODIC TABLE
1 a) individual e.g. oxygen, aluminium, iron; b) oxygen or nitrogen; c) mercury; d) iodine

2 a) carbon, b) copper, c) mercury, d) carbon, e) iron, f) helium

3 diagram of atom (see p30)

4 a) oxygen, b) carbon, c) helium, d) fluorine

5 a) H, b) Cl, c) Fe, d) Pb

Unit 13 COMPOUNDS
1 CO_2, H_2O_2, H_2O

2 a) carbon, hydrogen, oxygen; b) 6 carbon atoms, 12 hydrogen atoms and 6 oxygen atoms

3 a) a compound is a chemical combination and a mixture is a physical combination; b) electrons

4

Iron	Water	Oxygen	Rust
solid, grey metal	Colourless, liquid	Colourless, odourless gas	Reddish – brown solid

5 a) bike chain – oiled; b) bike frame – painted; c) rack – plastic coating; d) iron roof – galvanised

Unit 14 OXYGEN – THE ELEMENT OF LIFE
1 O, odourless, 8th, respiration produces higher temperature, gas, colourless, in photosynthesis, needed for combustion, absorb UV

2 a) most living things need it to produce energy; b) from plants; c) the hole in the ozone layer is spreading over NZ which means more exposure to UV radiation and increased risk of skin cancer; d) ozone protects Earth from harmful UV radiation; e) chloroflourocarbons

3 a) atomic number, number of protons; b) atoms in one molecule of oxygen; c) the ozone layer is 15–50km above Earth; d) the temperature of an oxyacetylene flame

4 left door closed so no oxygen (air) got into the oven, then the fire would have gone out

Unit 15 HYDROGEN – AN EXPLOSIVE ELEMENT
1 all except helium

2 helium airship because helium does not explode and burn

3 order = B, E, F, D, A, G, C

4 a) hydrogen has only 1 proton so is very light; b) helium is light, and is is not flammable (unlike hydrogen); c) fertilisers are important to NZ because agriculture is a primary industry

5 individual e.g. doesn't use fossil fuels, no carbon dioxide produced, good for environment

Unit 16 CARBON DIOXIDE – FIZZ AND FOAM
1 (in order of right hand column then left hand column of table) CO_2, colourless, 0.04%, heavier than air, to dry ice, gas, odourless, does not burn, photosynthesis, affects global warming

2 carbon dioxide is a compound because it is made of 2 chemical elements that have been chemically combined

3 plants take in carbon dioxide to use in photosynthesis; plants and animals release carbon dioxide during respiration

4 individual e.g. trigger (squeeze to release gas); cylinder (contains gas under pressure)

5 a) it is non-flammable and is heavier than air so smothers fires; b) the carbon dioxide that was put in the water under pressure escapes when the top is opened; c) yeast produce carbon dioxide during fermentation and this makes the bread rise; d) there are not liquid puddles to clean up afterwards and no liquid to damage food or medicine; e) to stop global warming getting worse

6 a) cutting down trees – trees take in carbon dioxide for use in photosynthesis; fewer trees means less carbon dioxide removed from atmosphere; b) aerosol cans – propellant CFCs once used destroy the ozone layer which allows more radiation to enter Earth's atmosphere; c) and d) cars and factories – burning of fossil fuels adds carbon dioxide to atmosphere

Unit 17 PLASTICS – THE MATERIAL OF OUR TIME
1 individual e.g. bowls, milk bottles, pens

2 a) carbon and hydrogen; b) thermoplastics can be repeatedly softened by heating and hardened by cooling which allows them to be recycled; thermosetting plastics are initially soft but change irreversibly to a hard rigid form so cannot be reshaped and reused

3 advantages = made from natural plant polymers, can be

broken down by micro-organisms in soil; disadvantages = more expensive to make and buy so people don't use them

4 advantages = stronger, lighter, last longer; disadvantages = take a long time to break down and decompose, contribute to a 'throw away society'

5 number refers to type of plastic it is and therefore how it can be recycled

TOPIC 3 ENERGY ALL AROUND US

Unit 18   What is energy?

1 energy makes things happen; energy can be changed from one form into another; the sun produces heat and light energy

2 individual e.g. light, heat, kinetic, sound

3 a) heat and light; b) light and heat; c) sound

4 a) 15kJ, b) 600kJ, c) 7.5kJ

5 chemical potential into kinetic, sound, heat

6 renewable = geothermal, hydroelectric, solar, wind; they do not use up Earth's limited resources: non renewable = coal, oil, natural gas; there is a limited amount and that will run out

Unit 19   FORMS OF ENERGY

1 a) chemical, b) electrical, c) wind

2

sound	gravitational/ potential	elastic
elastic	light	kinetic/ gravitational
nuclear	electrical	chemical potential

3 a) stored, b) nuclear, c) light, d) electrons, e) kinetic, f) kinetic

4 a) car travelling at 80km/hr; b) bowling ball rolling along a path

5 1 sitting at top of slide

6 ice cream, bread, soft drink, chocolate bar, French fries

Unit 20   ENERGY TRANSFERRED AND TRANSFORMED

1 individual

2 a) there has been no change in energy as it has moved from one place/object to another; b) the energy has changed from one form to another as it has moved from one place/object to another.

3

Example	Energy in	Energy out
child sliding down slide	gravitational potential	kinetic, heat
torch	chemical potential	light, heat, electrical
solar powered calculator	light from sun	light, electrical
archer shooting an arrow	elastic potential	kinetic, heat
leaf of a plant	light	chemical potentail
a fire	chemical potential	light, heat
light bulb	electrical	light, heat

4 a) individual e.g. i) transistor radio; ii) plant, leaf; iii) game boy; iv) person; b) i) chemical to sound; ii) electrical to heat and light; iii) elastic to kinetic; iv) chemical to kinetic, sound and heat

5 a) all of it (energy cannot be created or destroyed); b) energy in equals energy out

Unit 21   EFFICIENCY AND POWER

1 a) heat, b) efficiency, c) power

2 useful – heat, light, light; waste – light, heat, heat

3 3/60 ×100 = 5%

4 a) 100 joules, b) 10 000 joules

5 radio pie chart – 60% sound and 40% heat; 60 watt light bulb – 10% light, 90% heat (using table) or 5% light 95% heat if using answer from q3

Unit 22   THE ENERGY OF FOOD

1 a) John = 0.25 x 800 = 200kJ; b) Sarah = 0.25 x 1 250 = 312.5kJ

2 a) 0.75 x 840 = 630kJ; b) 100g grain =1260kJ so Steven needs to eat 200g of grain

3 100g chicken (1260kJ), 100g potato (378 kJ) = 1638kJ food energy; walking uses 800 kJ per hour so Jamie needs to walk about 2 hours

4 a) 673 – 479 = 194 kJ; b) bike – 0.25 x 1250 = 312.5 kJ, run – 0.25 x 1600 = 400kJ, light work – 3 x 600 = 1800; Total for day = 2512.5kJ; c) 2512.5/479 = 5.25 servings

5 to keep our body at constant temperature

Unit 23   NON-RENEWABLE ENERGY SOURCES

1 a) non-renewable means there is a limited supply so fuel will eventually run out; b) made from the remains of dead plants and animals that died millions of years ago; c) expense involved in building power stations, danger of leaking radiation

2 oil – heating, lubrication, made into petrol, diesel, kerosene; natural gas – heating, cooking

3 a) renewable, b) kerosene, c) Marsden Point, d) gas

4 pie chart to show – 10% for power generation, 10% for industrial energy, 25% for steel production, 5% for commercial heating, 5% for domestic heating and 45% for export

5 pie chart – 45% bituminous, 49% sub bituminous, 6% lignite

Unit 24   ENERGY FOR THE FUTURE – RENEWABLE ENERGY SOURCES

1 hydroelectric, wind, hydrogen (chemical), geothermal, solar, biomass, wave, biogas, coal

2 a) many sources of energy are running out; b) more large rivers

3 hydroelectric, geothermal

4 a) advantages – cheaper, burns more cleanly, more efficient, has own supplies; b) it is an alternative energy source

Unit 25   An Example of Energy production in NZ

1 a) windy on lots of days; b) it is cheap, clean alternative energy readily available; c) some people think they are ugly and spoil environment

2 non-scientific

3 a)

N
W ┼ E   b) south of NZ; c) south of Manukau
S   Harbour; d) individual; e) big

Unit 26   The Third Rock from the Sun

1 a) A sun with planets, moons, (asteroids, meteorites, comets) that orbit it; b) labels – Mercury, Venus, (Earth), Mars, Jupiter, Saturn, Uranus, Neptune, Pluto.

2 water and oxygen (and warm temperature)

3 a) 24 hours; b) day and night occur; c) 365$\frac{1}{4}$ days (1 year); d) a leap year has an extra day to bring calendar back in line with movement of Earth around sun, makes up for the quarter days; e) tilt of axis in relation to its orbital path and the fact Earth moves around the sun

4 Crust – mainly oxygen and silicon minerals, 5–40 km thick; Mantle – molten rock, 1300–2000°C; Outer and inner core – semi-solid and solid, iron and nickel, 3000–5000°C

5 Spring = September; Summer = December; Winter = June; Autumn = March

6 labels as page 66

7 a) Shortest day – June 21st/22nd; Longest day – December 21st/22nd b) short – when South Pole is tilted away from the sun, long – when Pole is tilted towards the sun

Unit 27   THE MOON – EARTH'S NATURAL SATELLITE

1 a) the moon has less mass, is smaller than the Earth; b) it reflects sunlight; c) the sun is on the opposite side of the moon to the Earth so it lights up the side we cannot see; d) the sun and the Earth are on the same side so the sun lights up the side of the moon we can see

2 a) individual; b) rock samples from the moon are similar in composition to those of Earth

3 a) individual, students copy diagrams p68 and 69

4 a) tides are caused by gravitational pull of moon and (to lesser extent) the sun; b) a Spring tide is bigger than a Neap tide because they occur when the moon and sun are pulling oceans in the same direction so there is more pull; in a Neap tide the sun and moon pull oceans at 90° to each other so the overall affect is less

Unit 28   SPACE EXPLORATION – THE INNER PLANETS VENUS AND MARS

1 a) a space probe is an unmanned spacecraft that carries instruments to record information about planets, moons and so on; b) individual e.g. huge distances that probes travel and the time it takes, the danger of entering unknown atmospheres; c) temperature on planet surface, composition of atmosphere, chemical composition of soil and rocks, photographs of surface features

2 temperature too hot 450°C, atmospheric pressure would crush us (90 times that of Earth), sulphuric acid in clouds and carbon dioxide main gas in the air

3 individual e.g. clouds of acid, volcanoes and mountain ranges

4 individual e.g. red colour, ice cap at pole, sky pinkish

5 1964 – Mariner 4; 1971- Mariner 9; 1976 – Viking 1 and 2; 1997 – Pathfinder and Global Surveyor; 2001 Mars Odyssey; 2003 Mars Explorer; 2005 Mars Reconnaissance Orbiter; 2007 Phoenix

6 a) ice, frozen water, channels where water may have flowed; b) close enough to get to within 12 months, temperature at poles 20°C, possibility of water, carbon dioxide in air so plants can grow

Unit 29   SPACE EXPLORATION – THE OUTER PLANETS – JUPITER, SATURN, URANUS, NEPTUNE

1 a) takes several years for probes to get to the outer planets b) the outer planets all lined up on the side of the sun c) Huygens probe

2 individual

3

Planet				
Name of planet	Jupiter	Saturn	Uranus	Neptune
Year Voyager passed	1979	1981	1986	1989
Temperature	−145°C	−115°C	−215°C	−215°C
Main gas in atmosphere	hydrogen	hydrogen	hydrogen	hydrogen
Moons	39	30	20	8

4 both are gaseous planets, not solid; both are made mainly of hydrogen and helium; both are very cold; both have several moons

5 too cold, planets are not solid but gaseous or liquid, no breathable atmosphere, too far away

Unit 30   SATELLITES

1 artificial satellites are man-made and natural satellites are things like moons

2 a) less interference by dust in atmosphere; b) they re-enter Earth's atmosphere and are pulled at high speeds towards Earth; c) it is safer than falling onto land, not needed any more; d) they move at the same speed and in the same direction as the Earth as it rotates on its axis

Unit 31   GLOBAL POSITIONING SYSTEM

1 a) GPS – Global Positioning System; b) Navstar – Navigation Satellite Tracking and Ranging; c) your position on Earth (accurate to within 10m); your altitude; your speed and direction of travel; the time where you are; d) a space segment (satellite), a controller segment (military base) and a user segment (receiver); e) can get to scene of emergency faster because closest; f) individual eg used by trampers and hunters, used by AA road rescue

Unit 32   SPACE TRAVEL – LIVING IN SPACE

1 a) 16 countries are involved in building it; b) to carry out experiments such as growing plants in micro gravity, looking at the effects of micro gravity on the human body

2 extremes of temperature – heat shields protect spacecraft; high levels of radiation – window filters, space suits reflect radiation, large doses of vitamins; space junk – double hulled spacecraft; harmful effects on the body – medication, exercise, dietary supplements

Unit 33   SPACE SPINOFFS

1 individual

2 individual

1   Name 5 things made from plastics you use in your home.

a) _____   b) _____   c) _____

d) _____   e) _____

2   Give answers to these questions.

a) What chemical elements are plastics often made from? _____

b) What is the difference between thermoplastics and thermosetting plastics? _____

_____

_____

3   Fill out the chart on biodegradable plastics.

Advantages	Disadvantages

4   Fill out the chart.

Advantages of plastics	Disadvantages of plastics

5   Draw one symbol that shows that plastics can be recycled and find out what the different numbers inside mean.

6   Write down 3 things you have learned from this unit.

a) _____

b) _____

c) _____

7   Write down anything you need to ask your teacher to explain.

_____

DIFFERENT FORMS OF ENERGY

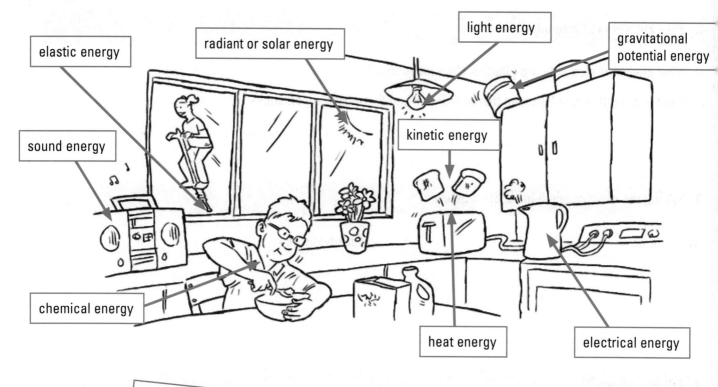

elastic energy

radiant or solar energy

light energy

gravitational potential energy

sound energy

kinetic energy

chemical energy

heat energy

electrical energy

Energy exists in many forms.

You can see the things that are happening because of the energy an object possesses.

Scientists say energy is 'the ability to do work'.

This work could be jumping on a pogo stick, heating water in a kettle to make a cup of tea or a light bulb changing electrical energy into light energy.

Energy makes things happen.

Energy itself is not something you can touch or see.

Energy is measured in joules (J). A joule is a very small unit (about as much energy as it takes to lift this book 10cm off the table). So scientists use kilojoules (kJ) instead.

1 kilojoule = 1000 joules.

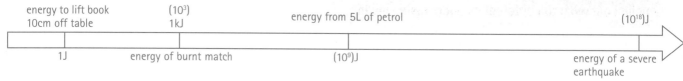

energy to lift book 10cm off table

(10^3)
1kJ

energy from 5L of petrol

(10^{18})J

1J

energy of burnt match

(10^9)J

energy of a severe earthquake

Energy can be changed from one form to another. In the drawing above there are many appliances using electrical energy. But they are transforming it into several other types of energy e.g. the radio is transforming electrical energy into sound energy.

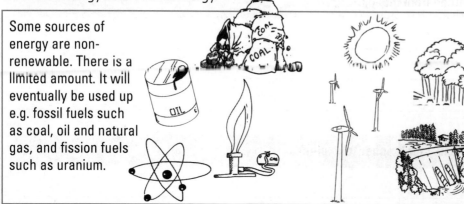

Some sources of energy are non-renewable. There is a limited amount. It will eventually be used up e.g. fossil fuels such as coal, oil and natural gas, and fission fuels such as uranium.

Other sources of energy are renewable. This means they do not use up Earth's limited resources e.g. wood (biomass), geothermal energy, hydroelectric energy, nuclear fusion, solar energy, tides, wind power and wave power.

1   Circle the correct statements below.

a) Energy makes things happen.

b) Energy is a substance like matter.

c) The sun produces heat and light energy.

d) Fossil fuels are a renewable energy source.

e) Energy can be changed from one form into another.

2   Write down the names of 3 forms of energy at work in your room right now.

a) _____   b) _____   c) _____

3   Under the pictures below write the name of the energy being produced.

a) _____   b) _____   c) _____

4   There are 1000 joules in a kilojoule. Write the following energy values as kilojoules.

a) 15 000 J _____   b) 600 000 J _____   c) 7 500 J _____

5   The child is transforming one form of energy into 3 other forms of energy. Show this by labelling the boxes with the energy forms.

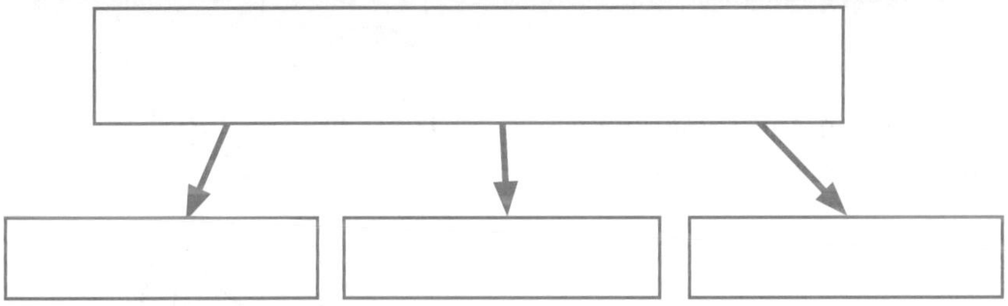

6   Complete the chart by giving 2 examples for each and showing the differences between renewable and non-renewable energy sources.

Renewable sources e.g _____ and _____	Non-renewable sources e.g _____ and _____

7   Write down 3 things you have learned from this unit.

a) _____

b) _____

c) _____

8   Write down anything you need to ask your teacher to explain.

_____

UNIT 19 — FORMS OF ENERGY

Most of our energy comes from the sun in the form of electromagnetic waves. It is used directly or transformed into other forms.

Light powers the process of photosynthesis in plants, which produces glucose, a form of chemical energy. The plant uses this energy to grow. When animals eat plants, they use the chemical energy in plants to grow. When plants and animals die, they decompose and can form fossil fuels such as coal and oil. These are also forms of energy.

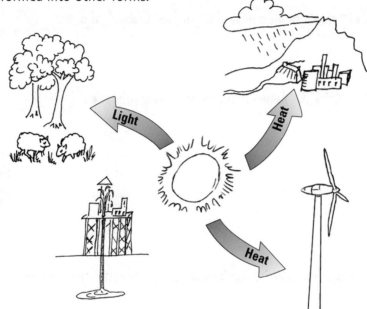

Heat is used to evaporate water from oceans and lakes, which forms clouds that produce rain. Rainwater is used in hydro-electric power stations to generate electrical energy.

Heat also causes winds to blow. Wind can turn the blades of wind turbines that then generate electrical energy. Wind can be used by yachts to sail across the water.

Energy can be divided into two main groups.

kinetic or active energy	stored or potential energy

KINETIC OR ACTIVE ENERGY INCLUDES

Light It comes from natural sources such as the sun and some living things such as glow-worms, and from artificial sources such as light bulbs and fireworks.

Sound Vibrating objects set up waves that travel through a medium such as air. The speed of sound waves through air is 330 metres per second.

Kinetic It is the energy associated with movement. An object's kinetic energy depends on its mass and how fast it is moving. A truck has more kinetic energy than a car when moving at the same speed.

Heat It causes the particles in matter to move more quickly. This causes matter to rise in temperature.

Electrical It is a result of electrons (negatively charged parts of atoms) flowing through a conductor.

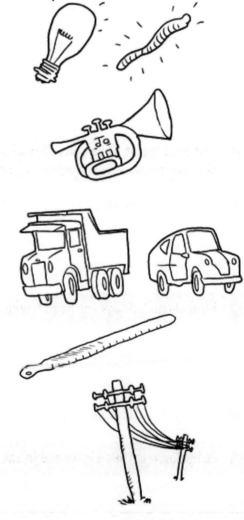

46

STORED OR POTENTIAL ENERGY INCLUDES:

Gravitational Any object raised above the ground has this type of energy. When the object falls or moves back towards the ground, this energy is transformed into other types of energy.

Elastic Springs and elastic bands can be squashed or stretched but then move back into their original shape, releasing their energy.

Nuclear The central part of an atom (the nucleus) can be split or joined to the nucleus of another atom releasing energy.

Chemical Fuels, including the food you eat, have energy stored in the chemical bonds that hold atoms together. This energy is released when the bonds are broken e.g. during respiration in living cells.

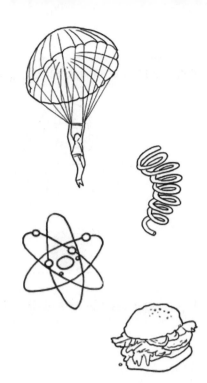

1 Name 3 forms of energy that are produced because the sun sends light and heat to earth.

a) _____ b) _____ c) _____

2 Name the form of energy in the following.

a) _____	b) _____	c) _____
d) _____	e) _____	f) _____
g) _____	h) _____	i) _____

3 Circle the correct answer for each of the following.

a) The word 'potential' in potential energy means i) active ii) stored iii) kinetic.

b) Energy released when the central part of an atom is split is i) nuclear ii) chemical iii) elastic.

c) An example of kinetic energy is i) gravitational ii) chemical iii) light.

d) Negatively charged parts of atoms are i) conductors ii) electrons iii) nuclei.

e) Heat is an example of i) active energy ii) kinetic energy iii) stored energy.

f) Music is an example of i) kinetic energy ii) light energy iii) elastic energy.

4U2DO

4 Circle which has more kinetic energy.

a)

50 km/hr    80 km/hr

b)

5 Circle who has most gravitational potential energy.

6 Food contains chemical potential energy. Foods high in carbohydrates (starches and sugars) and fats have higher energy values than foods low in these. In the following pairs, circle the one with the highest energy value (assume there is the same amount of each food).

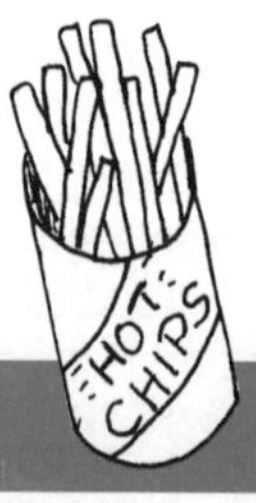

7 Write down 3 things you have learned from this unit.

a) _____

b) _____

c) _____

8 Write down anything you need to ask your teacher to explain.

_____

UNIT 20 — ENERGY TRANSFERRED AND TRANSFORMED

When you use a hot water bottle, the heat energy from it moves into you and you gain heat energy, which warms you up. There has been no change in energy as it has moved from the hot water bottle to you. So we say that energy has been **transferred**.

Another example of energy being transferred can be seen in the food chain below.

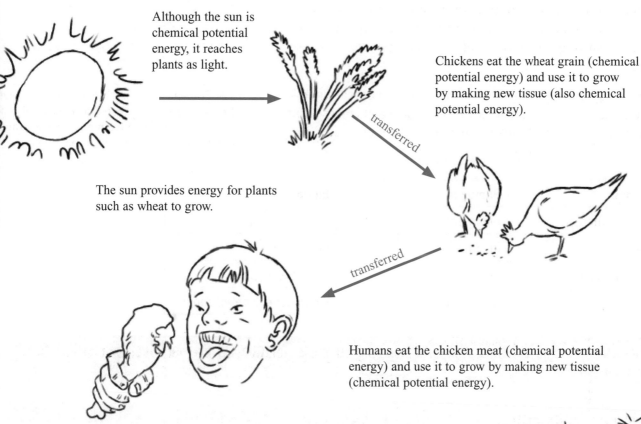

Although the sun is chemical potential energy, it reaches plants as light.

Chickens eat the wheat grain (chemical potential energy) and use it to grow by making new tissue (also chemical potential energy).

The sun provides energy for plants such as wheat to grow.

Humans eat the chicken meat (chemical potential energy) and use it to grow by making new tissue (chemical potential energy).

At two steps of the food chain some chemical potential energy from the previous step is used to make new chemical potential energy and some energy is lost as heat.

When you light the fuse on fireworks, chemical potential energy is changed into heat, light and sound energies. There has been a change in the form of energy so it is said the energy has been transformed.

A battery in a Gameboy contains chemical potential energy. This is changed into electrical energy, which is in turn changed into light and sound energy. There is also some heat energy produced as the wires carrying the electrical energy heat up.

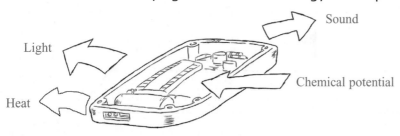

Sound

Light

Heat

Chemical potential

Your body transforms the chemical potential energy in the food you eat into:

- heat energy to keep your body at a constant temperature
- kinetic energy as you move
- chemical potential energy into chemical potential energy that is stored in your cells.

The amount of chemical potential energy contained in your breakfast food is transformed into an equal amount of the other forms of energy. For example, a breakfast consisting of a bowl of cereal and milk provides about 1000kJ of chemical potential energy. Your body transforms most of this, during a special process called respiration, into heat energy but some is used in walking to school and making new cells to help you grow.

The energy source used most in homes is electrical energy. Electricity is used to run many household appliances that transform it into other forms of energy to make our daily lives easier.

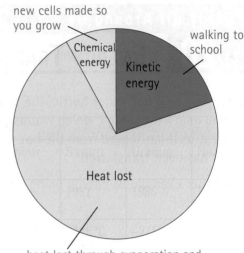

new cells made so you grow

Chemical energy

Kinetic energy

walking to school

Heat lost

heat lost through evaporation and keeping body at constant temperature

The Principle of Conservation of Energy says: **Energy cannot be created or destroyed but it can be transformed from one form to another** In other words – energy in = energy out.

Appliance	Energy in	Energy out
electric toothbrush	electrical	kinetic, sound
toaster	electrical	heat, light
washing machine	electrical	kinetic, sound
microwave	electrical	microwave, kinetic, sound

4U2DO

1 See who can come up with the longest list of things that use electricity. Write your list around the margins of this unit.

2 Complete the sentences.

a) **Energy is transferred when** _____

b) **Energy is transformed when** _____

3 Complete the table to show the energy transformations taking place.

Example	Energy in	Energy out
child sliding down slide		
a torch		
solar powered calculator		
archer shooting an arrow		
leaf of a plant		
a fire		
a light bulb		

4 a) In the 4 blank boxes, draw or name something that carries out the energy changes shown.

i) Chemical ⟶ light, sound, heat	ii) Light ⟶ chemical potential
iii) Electrical ⟶ light, sound, heat	iv) Chemical ⟶ kinetic, heat

b) Write the energy changes that these machines produce.

  i)	 ii)
  iii)	 iv)

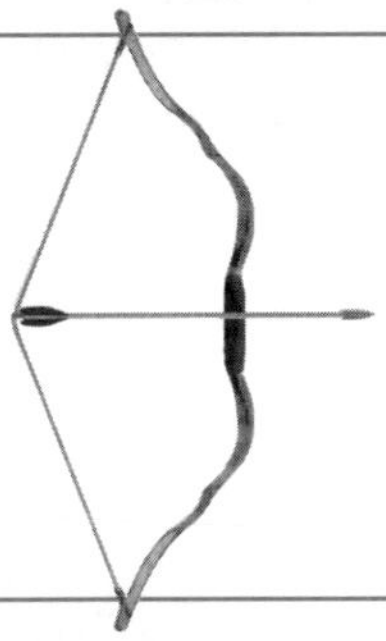

5 Find answers to the questions.

a) How much of the energy going into an appliance is transformed into other forms of energy?

_____

b) What 5 words summarise the Principle of Conservation of Energy?

_____

6 Write down 3 things you have learned from this unit.

a) _____

b) _____

c) _____

7 Write down anything you need to ask your teacher to explain.

_____

UNIT 21 EFFICIENCY AND POWER

The petrol put into a car is a form of chemical potential energy.

The car's engine transforms this energy to make the car move (kinetic energy). This is useful energy.

The car's engine also transforms this energy into heat and sound. These are waste energies.

How much useful energy a machine such as a car engine produces is called its efficiency. For every 100 joules of chemical energy (petrol) put into a car only 25 joules appear as useful kinetic energy. The rest is waste energy mainly in the form of heat. A car engine is only 25% efficient.

lost as heat

75J

100J (petrol)

25J movement of car

$$\text{Energy efficiency (\%)} = \frac{\text{Useful energy output}}{\text{Total energy input}} \times 100$$

Many of the household appliances that make our lives easier are not very efficient at transforming electrical energy into useful energy.

Appliance	Energy transformed (joules per second)	Useful energy out (J/s)	Efficiency	Waste energy
toaster	electrical 1400 J/s	heat 400 J/s	29%	light
electric kettle	electrical 2400 J/s	heat 1600 J/s	67%	sound, kinetic
60W light bulb	electrical 60 J/s	light 6 J/s	10%	heat
radio	electrical 50 J/s	sound 30 J/s	60%	heat

The human body is no more efficient at transforming energy than many machines or appliances. An athlete uses up 40 000 joules of chemical (food) energy sprinting 100m. Only 8000J of this is converted into the kinetic energy of running. 32 000J is wasted as heat energy.

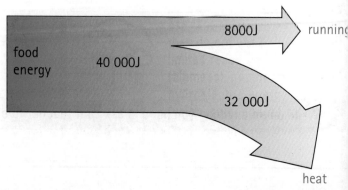

food energy 40 000J

8000J running

32 000J

heat

The amount of energy transformed by a machine every second is called the power of the machine. Power is measured in watts (1 watt = 1 joule of energy transformed every second).

Light bulbs and microwaves come in a variety of wattages (power). The wattage information is on a label on the bulb and microwave.

A 60-watt light transforms 60 joules of electrical energy into light and heat every second.

A 100-watt light bulb transforms 100 joules of electrical energy into light and heat every second.

This means the 100-watt bulb will produce more light than the 60 watt bulb.

A 650 watt microwave transforms 650 joules of electrical energy into microwave energy every second.

A 1000 watt microwave transforms 1000 joules of electrical energy into microwave energy every second.

Food will cook faster in the more powerful microwave.

1 Answer the questions about Science Rulz.

a) What is the main form of waste energy

produce by Science Rulz? _____

b) What term is used for how much useful energy

Science Rulz produces? _____

c) What term is used for the amount of energy

transformed by Science Rulz per second?

_____

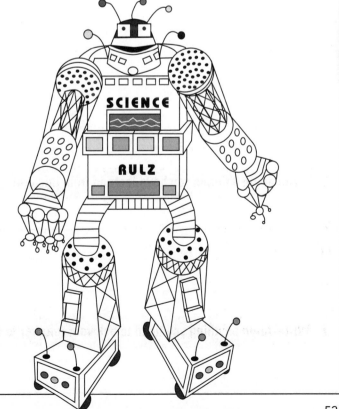

2 For each appliance below underline or highlight the useful energy produced and circle the waste energy.

HEAT LIGHT

HEAT LIGHT

HEAT LIGHT

3 Use the formula on page 52 to help you calculate the efficiency of this light bulb.

> In 1 second a 60-watt light bulb transforms 3 joules of electrical energy into light and 57 joules into heat.

_____

4 An electric lamp is labelled as 100 watts. How many joules of energy are transformed into heat and light:

a) **every second?** _____

b) **over a period of 100 seconds?** _____

5 In the spaces provided draw a pie chart to show the proportion of useful and waste energy in the named appliances. Use the table in this unit to help you.

Radio

60 watt light bulb

6 Write down 3 things you have learned from this unit.

a) _____

b) _____

c) _____

7 Write down anything you need to ask your teacher to explain.

_____

UNIT 22 THE ENERGY OF FOOD

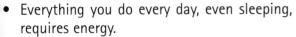

- Everything you do every day, even sleeping, requires energy.
- Different activities require different amounts of energy.

| J = joule kJ = kilojoule 1 kJ = 1,000 J |

How much energy your body needs each day
- is different for males and females
- changes with age and activity level (e.g. type of job, sport done)
- may be different for an individual on different days (e.g. you will need more energy on days you have PE or sports training than on days you do not).

Male or female, young or old, active or 'couch potato', people get the energy they need each day from the food they eat. This food is a form of chemical potential energy. When food is burned in the body's cells during respiration, the chemical potential energy is released.

Activity	kJ per hour
sleeping	200
sitting	300
light work	600
walking	800
active work	840
walking upstairs	1 000
cycling	1 250
running	1 600

Age	Daily energy needs of females (kilojoules)	Daily energy needs of males (kilojoules)
5 years	7000	7000
10 years	9000	10 000
15 years	9 500	13 000
20 years	9 500	12 500
25 years	9 000	11 500

Different foods release different amounts of energy.

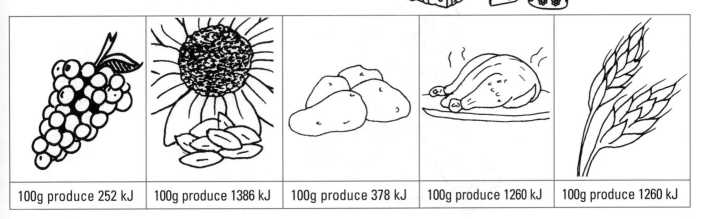

| 100g produce 252 kJ | 100g produce 1386 kJ | 100g produce 378 kJ | 100g produce 1260 kJ | 100g produce 1260 kJ |

To keep healthy and not become overweight	→	balance your energy input with your energy output.
To avoid problems such as blocked arteries and tooth decay	→	don't eat too much fatty or sugary foods.

Walk to school, netball practice, dance classes.

Bus to school, no PE today, watch TV.

All food packaging carries a table with nutritional information about that food. It lists the amount of protein, fat, and carbohydrates in an average serving as well as the energy contained in an average serving.

SERVINGS PER PACKAGE: 8 SERVING SIZE: 77g (73ml)	AVE. QUANTITY PER 77g SERVING	AVE. QUANTITY PER 100g
ENERGY	266kJ/64kcal	347kJ/83kcal
PROTEIN	LESS THAN 1g	LESS THAN 1g
FAT – TOTAL – SATURATED	LESS THAN 1g LESS THAN 1g	LESS THAN 1g LESS THAN 1g
CARBOHYDRATES – TOTAL – SUGARS	15.5g 15.5g	20.3g 20.3g
SODIUM	LESS THAN 5mg	LESS THAN 5mg

A large amount of the energy our bodies get from food is transformed into heat energy as a result of respiration. This is used to keep our bodies at a constant temperature (37°C). This is important if the chemical reactions that take place in the cells are to run efficiently.

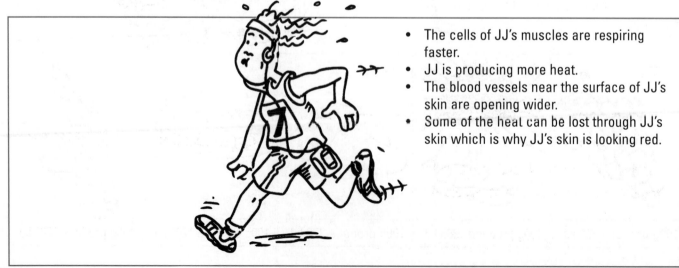

- The cells of JJ's muscles are respiring faster.
- JJ is producing more heat.
- The blood vessels near the surface of JJ's skin are opening wider.
- Some of the heat can be lost through JJ's skin which is why JJ's skin is looking red.

1   John takes 15 minutes to walk to school. Sarah takes 15 minutes to cycle to school. Calculate how much energy John and Sarah use to get to school. (Clue = you will have to work out what fraction of an hour each trip takes.) Use the table on page 55.

a) John _____

b) Sarah _____

2   Steven mows his parent's lawn on Saturdays. It takes him 3/4 of an hour.

a) How much energy does Steven use? _____

b) How many grams of grains does Steven need to eat to supply this amount of energy? _____

3   Jamie eats 100g of chicken and 100g of potato at lunch on Sunday. Approximately how many hours will he need to walk to use up the chemical energy supplied by his lunch?

_____

4   Check out the nutrition information on the cereal box of cereal that Hannah likes for breakfast.

	Average quantity per serving (30g or 1 metric cup))	Average quantity per serve with skim milk	Average quantity per 100g
Energy	479kJ	673kJ	1596kJ

a) How much extra energy does the skim milk provide to this breakfast? _____

b) Hannah has an active day ahead. Work out how much energy she will need for these 3 activities.

BIKING	RUNNING	WORKING IN SUPERMARKET
15 minutes = ... of an hour _____	15 minutes = ... of an hour _____	3 hours _____
Energy used _____	Energy used _____	Energy used _____

c) Work out how many average servings of cereal she would need to eat if this breakfast had to supply her entire

energy for the day _____

5   Answer this question.

What does our body use the heat energy it produces for? _____

6   Write down 3 things you have learned from this unit.

a) _____

b) _____

c) _____

7   Write down anything you need to ask your teacher to explain.

_____

UNIT 23 NON-RENEWABLE ENERGY SOURCES

Humans use energy at a rate of 1000 million, million, million joules every year. Fossil fuels such as coal, oil and natural gas are non-renewable. They were formed from the remains of plants and animals which died millions of years ago. They have a high carbon content. When carbon is burnt, energy is released. Nuclear energy sources such as uranium are also non-renewable. Earth has a limited supply of non-renewable forms of energy.

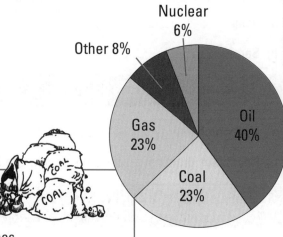

Energy supplied by non-renewable sources (%)

Coal

- provides 23% of the world's energy needs
- will last another 300 years at the present rate of use
- is the most abundant fossil fuel in New Zealand (3.3 million tonnes produced each year)
- is either lignite (Southland and central Otago), or bituminous/sub bituminous (West Coast) or anthracite (none mined in NZ)
- is found at different depths below the Earth's surface according to what type it is
- is mined by either deep shaft mining or open-cast mining.
- is used in NZ for power generation (10%) e.g. at the Huntly power station; for industrial energy (10%) for steel production (25%), for heating government buildings, schools and hospitals (5%), for domestic heating (5%) and for export (45%).

Petroleum oil

- provides 40% of the world's energy needs (77 million barrels of oil are used every day across the world)
- might have enough supplies to last another 30 years
- is largely found in Saudi Arabia, Kuwait, Iran and the Arab Emirates (they hold 1/2 of the world's oil supply)
- is found in NZ (there are many small oil fields in Taranaki)
- is used largely by the USA and Europe (if every country used as much as USA & Europe, the world's oil would last only 4 years)
- is used as a fuel
- is used to make plastics, paints, pesticides and cosmetics
- is refined from its crude state, in New Zealand at Marsden Point Refinery near Whangarei (this separates it into many useful substances such as diesel, aviation kerosene and petrol).

The disadvantages of coal, oil and natural gas = when they are burnt, they produce sulphur dioxide and carbon dioxide. When sulphur dioxide dissolves in rainwater, it forms acid rain. The carbon dioxide produced adds to the greenhouse effect.

Natural gas

- provides 23% of the world's energy needs
- is a mixture of gases that are mostly made up of carbon and hydrogen
- is usually found in porous (spongy) rocks underground
- is found in the Taranaki region of NZ (Maui, Kapuni, McKee fields)
- has a NZ production of over 7 000 million cubic metres per year but current gas reserves are estimated to run out in 2014
- burns hotter than coal and oil
- is used in NZ for electricity generation (36.2%), production of synfuels and methanol (44%), production of ammonia and urea (3.1%), industrial and commercial use (14.1%), residential (2.5%), transport (0.1%)
- can be liquefied to make Liquefied Petroleum Gas (LPG), which can be bottled and used in places that a gas pipeline cannot reach
- is used as Compressed Natural Gas (CNG) as a fuel by some cars.

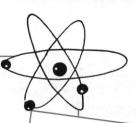

Nuclear power
- provides 6 % of the world's energy needs
- is used as a source of energy to generate electricity in nuclear power plants
- has uranium as the main source of nuclear energy
- Major disadvantages of nuclear power are
  - reactors are expensive to build
  - waste products must be disposed of safely
  - the risk of accidents releasing radiation that would poison the environment.

| 1kg of coal or oil can boil 80 litres of water. | 1 kg of nuclear fuel can boil 1 000 000 000 litres of water. |

ABOUT URANIUM
It is a silvery-white, radioactive metal (its nucleus breaks apart to release energy). It occurs in rocks in extremely small concentrations. 34 500 metric tons are produced annually (Canada is the main producer).

1 Answer these.

a) What is meant by the term 'non-renewable energy resource'?

_____

b) Why are coal, oil and natural gas called 'fossil' fuels?

_____

c) What problems need to be overcome before nuclear energy can be more widely used in the world?

_____

2 In the table record some uses for each of the energy sources

Oil	Natural gas

3 Cross out the items that least belong in the following lists to leave 3 items in each list.

a) renewable, non-renewable, uranium, nuclear energy

b) lignite, anthracite, kerosene, bituminous

c) Marsden Point, Maui, McKee, Kapuni

d) radioactive, gas, uranium, metal

4 Coal is New Zealand's most abundant fossil fuel. Draw a pie chart to show uses of coal in NZ.

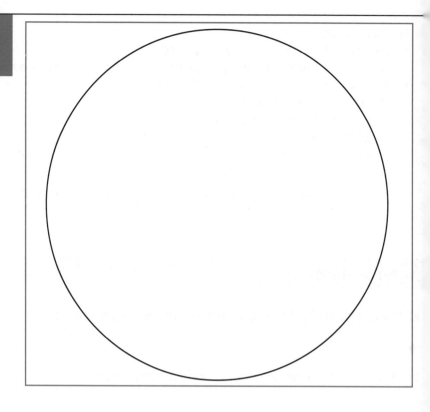

5 Draw a pie diagram to illustrate the following figures for coal.

In New Zealand 45% of coal is bituminous mined on the West Coast of the South Island, 49% is sub bituminous mined mostly in the Waikato and 6% is lignite mined in Southland and Otago.

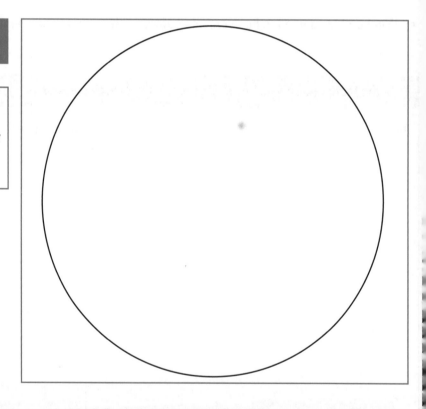

6 Write down 3 things you have learned from this unit.

a) _____

b) _____

c) _____

7 Write down anything you need to ask your teacher to explain.

_____

UNIT 24 ENERGY FOR THE FUTURE – RENEWABLE ENERGY SOURCES

Non-renewable energy resources are running out. The world constantly looks for alternative energy sources that are non-polluting, safe and renewable. Some have been used for many years. Some are still in the experimental stage. Most are used to generate electrical energy but some are used in their original form.

Alternative energy sources include

Solar Energy

- It comes from the sun in the form of electromagnetic waves. The amount the Earth receives in a year is more than enough to supply the entire world's energy needs for that year.
- Solar panels on the roofs of houses use solar energy to heat water.
- Solar cells are used in watches and calculators. They use solar energy to produce a small electric current.
- Panels of solar cells are used to produce the electricity needed by telecommunications satellites and space capsules orbiting the Earth.
- A solar furnace in Southern France collects enough energy to melt metals. It uses a giant curved mirror to collect sunlight from a series of smaller mirrors.
- Solar ovens use a concave mirror to focus the sun's rays on a pan for cooking.

Geothermal Energy

- Where hot rocks lie near the earth's surface, water trapped between rock layers is turned into steam by the heat energy inside the earth.
- The steam is used in power stations to generate electricity.
- Around 5% of New Zealand's electricity demand is met by geothermal generation.
- The main NZ geothermal generation is in Wairakei (near Taupo).

Biomass

- This is organic material that is converted into an energy source.
- Wood is a form of biomass. Burning wood chips produces a gas that is burned to release energy that can be used to provide heating or be used for electricity generation.
- In Brazil, sugar cane is used to produce alcohol that is then used to run cars instead of petrol.
- In the US, petrol is mixed with a fuel (alcohol) made from grain, sugar cane and potatoes. It is called Gasohol.

Tidal Energy

- Tides are caused by the gravitational pull of the Moon.
- A dam across an estuary can hold water, then use it to generate electricity.
- Tidal power stations are found in France, Canada and Northern Russia.

Hydro-electric Energy

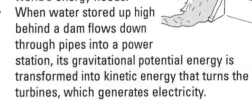

- It provides 7% of the world's energy needs.
- When water stored up high behind a dam flows down through pipes into a power station, its gravitational potential energy is transformed into kinetic energy that turns the turbines, which generates electricity.
- Around 60% of New Zealand's electricity demand is met by hydro-electric energy. Over 2/3 of hydro-electricity is generated in the South Island.

Wind Energy

- Air movement (wind) is the result of unequal heating of the earth's surface by the sun.
- Wind turbines turn in the wind and generate electricity.
- In New Zealand wind energy supplies enough electricity for more than 50 000 houses and this keeps increasing as new farms are built.

Biogas

- Decomposing plants, animals, rubbish and sewage produce biogas.
- When biogas combines with carbon dioxide, it produces methane. The process occurs in a closed container called a digester.
- In India and China this method is used to produce fuel for cooking.

Wave Energy

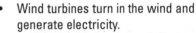

- Waves are caused by the wind blowing across sea.
- Large floats that move up and down with the waves are now being used to generate electricity.

Hydrogen

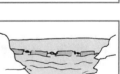

- It is used in fuel cells (see page 36)
- It can be combined with oxygen to generate an electric current.
- It burns easily releasing large amounts of heat energy.

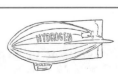

1 Name each type of energy shown.

		 PEM

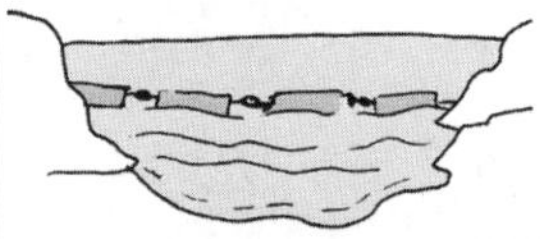	 DIGESTER	 Huntly Power Station

2 Give reasons for the following.

a) It is necessary to find new sources of energy. _____

b) Most of New Zealand's hydro-electric power stations are in the South Island.

_____

3 Name the forms of renewable energy most commonly used in New Zealand to generate electricity.

_____

4 Read the following recent news report and answer the questions.

A Brazilian aircraft manufacturer has unveiled the world's first mass-produced commercial aircraft that runs on sugar-cane ethanol fuel. Brazil has supplies of the fuel. It is cheaper, burns more cleanly and is more efficient than fuels refined from crude oil. It is 3 to 4 times cheaper than aviation fuel.

a) List advantages of ethanol fuel for Brazil.

i) _____ ii) _____

iii) _____ iv) _____

b) For what statement in the first paragraph of this unit does the extract serve as an example?

_____

5 Write down 3 things you have learned from this unit.

a) _____

b) _____

c) _____

6 Write down anything you need to ask your teacher to explain.

_____

25 AN EXAMPLE OF ALTERNATIVE ENERGY PRODUCTION IN NZ

New Zealand is fairly windy because it is exposed to westerly airflows from the Southern Ocean. Winds are strongest in exposed coastal and mountain areas and where the wind can be channelled though gaps in hill ranges. These are the areas where the wind farms have been built or are planned to be built. Together, New Zealand's wind farms produce many megawatts of electrical energy (1 megawatt = 1 million watts). That is enough energy to meet the needs of many thousands of households.

hau = wind in Maori

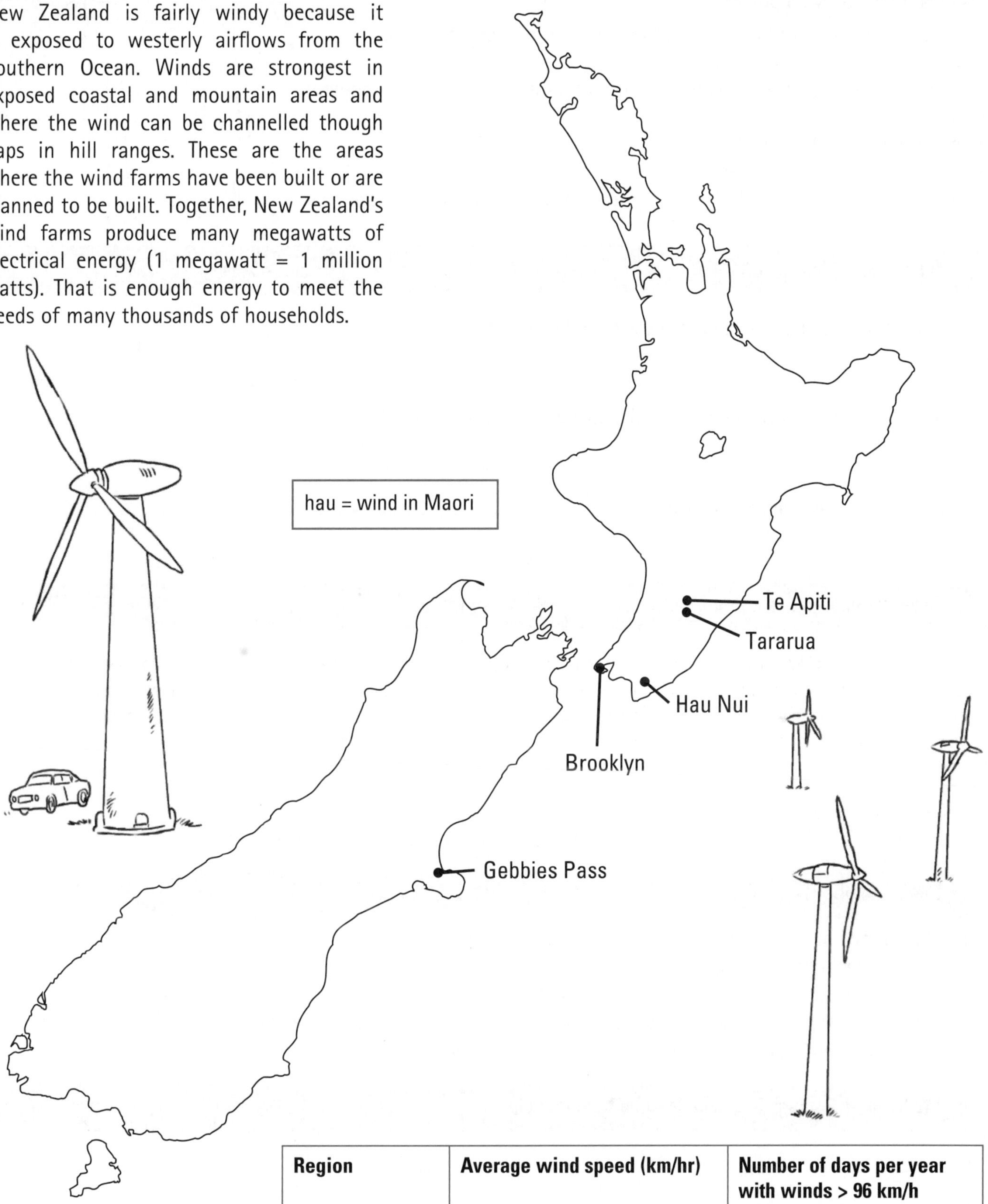

Te Apiti

Tararua

Hau Nui

Brooklyn

Gebbies Pass

Region	Average wind speed (km/hr)	Number of days per year with winds > 96 km/h
New Plymouth	19.8	5.5
Wellington	26.6	36.0
Christchurch	14.4	2.5
Invercargill	16.9	14.4

Advantages of wind power:
- is renewable   • no chemical pollution
- does not add to the greenhouse effect.

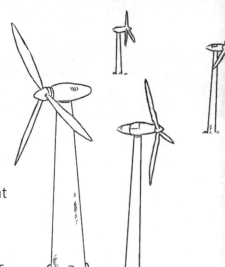

Disadvantages of wind power:
- needs many large turbines over a large area to produce as much electricity as one power station
- some people think the turbines spoil the natural look of the environment
- noisy
- needs wind to blow most days
- could affect Maori archaeological sites
- movement and shadow flicker from the blades could scare stock animals.

4U2DO

1   Give reasons for the following.

a) The Wellington region is a good place to build wind farms _____

_____

b) New Zealand should be looking at wind farms as a source of electricity _____

_____

c) Wind farms is a controversial issue _____

_____

2   Read the information about a recent controversial wind issue.

Awhitu Peninsula is 7km west of the small south Auckland town of Waiuku. It is windy. Genesis Energy tested 3 sites on it for a possible wind farm. It decided to build 19 90m-high wind turbines on the Peninsula. The wind farm would generate enough energy to supply 8,000 homes. Some people objected. Neighbours near the proposed wind farm said it would spoil views, hurt tourism and frighten horses at equestrian facilities. Maori claimed strong historical connection with the area. They said the wind farm would damage the landscape and Maori archaeological sites.

Circle the correct answer:
The objections to the wind farm are mainly i) *scientific issues* ii) *non-scientific issues.*

3   Check out the map and:

a) add a direction finder to show where westerlies come from
b) show the location of the Southern Ocean
c) show the location of Te Awhitu Peninsula out of Auckland
d) show where you live and add a note beside it saying whether or not the area would be suitable for a wind farm
e) write above the Maori word 'nui' what it could mean in English.

4   Write down 3 things you have learned from this unit.

a) _____

b) _____

c) _____

5   Write down anything you need to ask your teacher to explain.

_____

UNIT 26 — THE THIRD ROCK FROM THE SUN

Scientists believe Earth

- is 4.6 billion years old
- was formed along with the rest of our solar system when a cloud of gas and dust in space cooled and condensed.

> **Solar system** = sun and planets that orbit sun, and their moons

Earth is the third of 9 planets moving around the sun. The sun is a medium sized star. It is one of billions of stars that make up the Milky Way Galaxy. There are billions of galaxies in the Universe.

Earth is a sphere (ball) due to gravity pulling all matter towards the centre.

As a result of its spin, Earth is slightly fatter around the equator (40 075 km) than it is from North Pole to South Pole (40 008 km).

Earth travels (at 107 000 km/hr) around the sun in an elliptical path. This means it is not always the same distance from the sun. One orbit of the sun takes 365 1/4 days (1 year) and is 940 million kilometres long.

70% of the Earth's surface is covered by water, which is needed by all living things. Water reflects blue light. This is why Earth appears blue from space.

Earth spins (at 1666 km/hr) around an imaginary line that runs from North to South. This line is called the axis. Earth rotates towards the east. One rotation takes about 24 hours and is called a solar day.

Earth's atmosphere contains oxygen (20%) and carbon dioxide (<1%). Without them, there would be no plant or animal life as we know it.

Earth does not sit straight up and down. The axis is tilted at an angle of 23 1/2° to the pathway Earth follows around the sun.

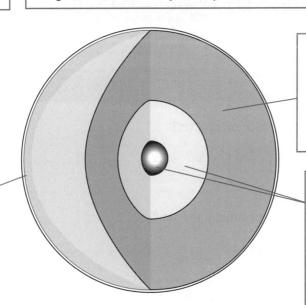

The mantle is thick molten rock (1300°–2000°C). It flows slowly because the core heats it. This causes the plates that float on it to move. One result of this movement is earthquakes.

Earth consists of a thin outer crust made up of about 30 pieces called tectonic plates. The continental crust is on average 40 km thick. The oceanic crust is 5 km thick. The crust is made up of minerals that are mainly combinations of the elements oxygen and silicon.

The outer (semi-liquid) and inner cores (solid due to pressure) are made mainly of iron and nickel. The temperature is thought to be 3000°C–5000°C. That is almost as hot as the surface of the sun but pressure keeps the core solid.

The tilt of Earth on its axis and the fact that Earth moves around the sun cause the seasons to change about every three months in many parts of the world. Changes in season are less dramatic near the equator where Earth bulges out and more noticeable near the Poles.

In New Zealand's summer, Earth is tilted so the southern hemisphere is towards the sun. Sunlight is more concentrated here. Sunlight is spread more thinly in the Northern Hemisphere where it will be winter.

In New Zealand's winter, the southern hemisphere experiences the weaker sunlight because the northern hemisphere is pointed toward the sun and having summer.

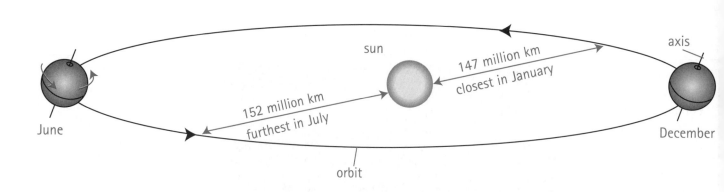

4U2DO

1 Finish the drawing by labelling the sun and 9 planets, and putting in the blank box an explanation of what a solar system is.

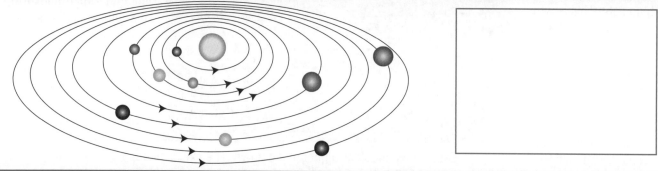

2 List the main features of Earth that make it possible for things to live here.

a) _____ b) _____ c) _____

3 Find answers to these questions.

a) How long does it take Earth to rotate once on its axis? _____

b) What do we notice happen over this period of time? _____

_____

c) How long does it take Earth to orbit once around the sun? _____

d) What is a leap year and why do we have one? _____

_____

e) What is the main reason the Earth experiences seasons? _____

_____

4 Label the three layers of Earth and write down one feature about each layer.

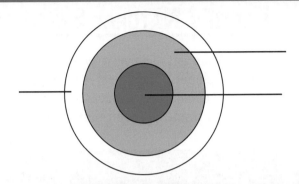

5 Under each season, put the date when the season begins in NZ.

SPRING

SUMMER

WINTER

AUTUMN

6 Finish the drawing by adding these labels in the right places (sun, Earth, equator, axis, orbit).

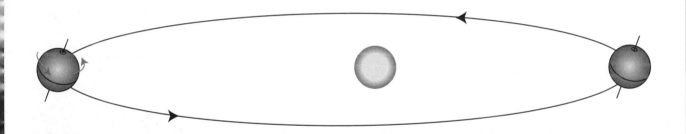

7 Find out:

a) when the shortest and longest days are in New Zealand. _____

b) what the position of the South Pole is in relation to the sun on these days. _____

8 Write down 3 things you have learned from this unit.

a) _____

b) _____

c) _____

9 Write down anything you need to ask your teacher to explain.

_____

27 THE MOON – EARTH'S NATURAL SATELLITE

The moon is our closest neighbour in space. Scientists believe it was also formed 4.6 billion years ago when Earth collided with a planet-sized object, sending a cloud of vaporised rock into orbit. This vaporised rock cooled and condensed to form the moon. Evidence for this comes from rock samples from the moon that are similar in composition to those of Earth.

Moves around the Earth travelling at 3 683 km per hour.

Average distance from Earth is 384 000 kilometres. The moon is moving away from Earth at a rate of 3.8 cm per year.

Gravity on the surface is 1/6th that of Earth because the moon has less mass than Earth. (Earth is about 81 times more massive.)

Equator temperatures range from −173 at night to 127°C during the day. But in some deep craters, the temperature stays around −240°C. There is evidence of frozen water in some of these craters.

The moon reflects the sunlight that hits its surface. As it orbits Earth, different amounts of the moon's lit side are visible from Earth. These changing areas reflecting light are called the **phases of the moon.**

It takes the moon 29 days 12 hours and 43 minutes to travel once around the Earth. This is called a **lunar month.**

The four phases of the moon are:

1 **New moon** – the moon is between the sun and Earth so the moon's lit side is away from Earth. We see a dark circle that is the moon being backlit.

2 **First quarter** – this occurs 7 days after the new moon or a quarter of the way through the month. Hence its name. Half the moon is lit.

3 **Full moon** – 7 days after the first quarter we see a fully lit moon. The moon is on the opposite side of Earth to the sun.

4 **Last quarter** – 7 days after a full moon or in the last quarter of the month another half moon is seen.

The word Lunar comes from the Latin word 'lunaris' meaning moon. Lunatic was the name given to people who showed strange behaviour, apparently due to the changing phases of the moon.

LUNAR MONTH			
1	2	3	4
NEW MOON	FIRST QUARTER	FULL MOON	LAST QUARTER

The moon is described as a **crescent** when it is smaller than half lit and as **gibbous** when it is more than half lit but not yet full. As the lit part of the moon increases, the moon is said to be **waxing**. As the lit part gets smaller, the moon is said to be **waning**. Occasionally two full moons occur within one calendar month. The second full moon is called a blue moon.

WAXING			WANING		
crescent	gibbous	full	gibbous	crescent	new

It takes the moon the same time (29$\frac{1}{2}$ days) to turn once on its axis (a lunar day) as it does to travel once around the Earth (a lunar month). For this reason there is one side of the moon, the far side, that is never seen from Earth. Pictures of the far side taken from space, show that it looks the same as the near side that we can see with binoculars.

The gravitational attraction of the moon on Earth is the main cause of ocean tides. The pull of the sun also has an effect on the tides but its pull is only half that of the moon because the sun is so far away from Earth and the moon is relatively close.

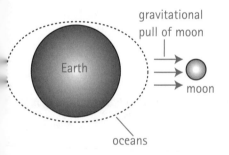

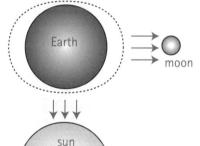

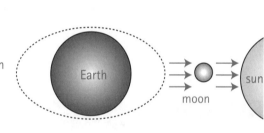

The moon pulls the water towards it causing a high tide (bulge) on the side of Earth closest to the moon. Another bulge forms on the other side of Earth where the moon's pull is weaker. This is a result of Earth's spin.

When the sun and the moon are pulling on Earth at right angles to each other, during the first and last quarters of a month, tides are smaller than usual. They are called **neap tides**.

When the sun, moon and Earth are in a line, during the full moon and new moon phases, larger than normal tides occur. These are called **spring tides**. They are caused by the sun and the moon's gravitational pull working together.

1 Give a reason for the following.

a) There is less gravity on the moon than there is on Earth. _____

_____

b) We can see the moon in the sky. _____

_____

c) A new moon appears to be a black circle in the sky. _____

_____

d) A full moon appears to be a brightly lit-up circle in the sky. _____

_____

4U2DO

2 Making the moon.

a) Put sketches in the top 3 boxes to show the 3 main steps that scientists believe took place during the formation of the moon.

1	2	3

b) Put in the long box, the reason scientists believe the moon was formed at about the same time as Earth.

3 In the spaces provided, complete the series of diagrams and labels to show how the moon waxes and wanes over the course of a lunar month.

New moon		1st quarter			Gibbous		Crescent

4 Explain

a) what causes the Earth's tides. _____

_____

_____

b) why a spring tide is higher than a neap tide. _____

_____

_____

_____

5 Write down 3 things you have learned from this unit.

a) _____

b) _____

c) _____

6 Write down anything you need to ask your teacher to explain.

_____

UNIT 28 SPACE EXPLORATION – INNER PLANETS, VENUS & MARS

Space exploration helps us see Earth in relation to the rest of the universe.	Unmanned spacecraft (space probes) give us knowledge of solar system.
First space probe, *Luna 1*, flew past moon in 1959.	Some probes do jobs while flying past a planet.
Some probes do jobs by orbiting a planet.	Some large primary probes drop smaller secondary probes into the planet's atmosphere
Some probes land on the planet's surface.	Some probes take photos of planets, moons, comets and asteroids.
Some probes collect and send back to Earth data about planets	Data sent back is about atmosphere, surface temperatures, atmospheric pressure, chemical makeup of surface rock and dust.
Some probes map the surface to identify features such as volcanoes and craters.	Technological advances keep improving instruments on probes and making data they collect more detailed.

Examples of space probe journeys to Venus and information gathered:

1961–78 Venera 1-16 sent to Venus by Soviet Union (union made up of many smaller countries including Russia, now no longer exists), gather data while flying past, drop probes into atmosphere, put landing probes on surface
1962–73 Mariner 1, 2, 5, 10 (US) gather data as they fly past
1978 Pioneer Venus 1, 2 (US) use radar to map surface and drop atmospheric probes
1985 Vega 1, 2 (Soviet Union) land, take soil samples from surface
1990 Magellan (US) uses advanced radar to take high-resolution pictures of surface
2005 Venus Express is European Space Agency's first mission to Venus. To enter the orbit of Venus in 2006 and spend 550 Earth days mapping the surface.

Features of Venus:

- Surface temperature is 465°C.
- Surrounded by clouds of sulphuric acid.
- Atmosphere is mainly carbon dioxide.
- Air pressure is 90 times that of Earth.
- Flat plains containing volcanoes, mountain ranges (tallest of which is 11.3 km high), valleys and canyons (deepest is 1km deep).
- Craters caused by impact of asteroids.
- Ring-like crowns (coronae) formed when hot material from inside planet comes to surface.

Venus

Venus Express on a mapping mission to Venus.

Examples of space probe journeys to Mars and information gathered:

Much interest has been taken in Mars because scientists believe there may once have been life on it and people could one day live on it.

1964 Mariner 4 (US) takes first close-up pictures of Mars

1971 Mariner 9 (US) is first probe to orbit Mars, maps surface and photographs Phobos and Deimos, the two moons of Mars

1976–78 Viking 2 (US) orbits, sends back data, drops a 'lander' probe to send data to Earth until 1980

1976–80 Viking 1 (US) orbits, its 'lander' probe continues to send data until 1982

1997 Pathfinder (US) lands, releases Sojourner rover controlled from Earth and guided across surface to take photos and collect samples

1997 Global Surveyor (US) uses altimeter to map surface and infrared spectrometer to analyse chemical composition of surface and just below

2001 Mars Odyssey (US) orbits, carries instruments to look for water (2002 large amounts of water ice discovered just below surface near Martian South Pole)

2003 Mars Express (European Space Agency) into orbit to collect data on atmosphere, structure and geology

2005 launch of Mars Reconnaissance Orbiter (US) to enter orbit 2006 and send data for 2 years tracking changes in the Martian atmosphere, and look for more evidence of seas and hot springs, and 2008–10 to act as data relay station

2007 launch of Phoenix Probe (US) to land on Martian North Pole 2008 and dig into arctic terrain for evidence of habitable zone that could support microbial life

Features of Mars:

- Covered in iron-rich red dust.
- Channels and valleys exist on the surface suggesting water once flowed there. Enormous volcanoes; one (Mount Olympus) is 27 km high.
- Large amounts of ice a metre below the surface near the South Pole.
- Thin atmosphere mainly carbon dioxide.
- Temperature ranges from −125°C near poles to 20°C near equator. Average is −60°C.
- Sky pinkish as light is reflected off red dust in atmosphere.

Mars

Mars Sojourner exploring the surface of Mars.

4U2DO

1 Think about space probes.

a) What is a space probe? _____

b) Why are space probes unmanned? _____

c) Give three pieces of information space probes may collect about a planet.

i) _____

ii) _____

iii) _____

2 List 3 pieces of information about Venus that make it impossible for life as we know it to exist there.

a) _____

b) _____

c) _____

3 Draw and label a sketch of Venus that would help you describe what its features are like to a Year 6 student.

Features of Venus

4 Draw and label a sketch of Mars that would help you describe what its features are like to a Year 6 student.

Features of Mars

5 On the time line below mark in the names and years of the space probes that have collected information on Mars and are mentioned in this unit.

1964   1970   1980   1990   2000   2005

6 Answer these questions.

a) What has been found on Mars that indicates life may have existed there? _____

b) Why do scientists believe people could one day live on Mars? _____

7 Write down 3 things you have learned from this unit.

a) _____

b) _____

c) _____

8 Write down anything you need to ask your teacher to explain.

_____

UNIT 29 SPACE EXPLORATION – OUTER PLANETS OF JUPITER, SATURN, NEPTUNE, URANUS

The outer planets have been much harder to study because they are so much further away from Earth (over 600 million kilometres) than the inner planets (less than 100 million kilometres away).

Between 1979 and 1989 Jupiter, Saturn, Uranus and Neptune were all lined up on the same side of the sun. This happens only every 175 years. Probes were launched to take advantage of this situation.

Cassini mission

1977 Voyager 2 (US) launched
1979 Voyager 2 flies by and photographs Jupiter
1981 Voyager 2 flies by and photographs Saturn
1986 Voyager 2 flies by and photographs Uranus
1989 Voyager 2 flies by and photographs Neptune
1989 Galileo (US) launched; **1995** goes into orbit around Jupiter, releases probe into Jupiter's atmosphere and gathers data on its four largest moons
1997 Cassini – Huygens (US) launched; **2004** enters Saturn's orbit to gather information about Saturn's rings, moons and magnetic field
2005 Cassini drop Huygens probe into atmosphere of Titan, Saturn's largest moon.

Features of Jupiter:

*   Largest planet in solar system (318 times larger than Earth).
*   No solid surface but is made up mainly of liquid hydrogen and helium surrounded by gases.
*   Atmosphere is 86% hydrogen and 14% helium.
*   Great Red Spot is a storm on the surface.
*   Temperature is –145°C above clouds and increases towards planet surface.
*   Has 39 'moons' (largest are Io, Europa, Ganymede and Callisto).

Features of Saturn:

*   Has 7 rings made up of thousands of ringlets each made of ice particles.
*   A 'gas planet' made up of layers that include methane and ammonia under syrupy hydrogen and helium.
*   Atmosphere of hydrogen and helium gas.
*   Temperature is –175°C.
*   Has 30 'moons'.

Features of Uranus:

*   Surrounded by broad ring system of dust to boulder-sized pieces of ice.
*   Has 20 moons.
*   Temperature –216°C.
*   Atmosphere mostly hydrogen with some helium and methane.
*   Covered in blue-green clouds of methane crystals.
*   Tilted on its axis so pole points towards the sun.

Features of Neptune:

*   Temperature –215°C.
*   Atmosphere mainly hydrogen and helium.
*   Active volcanoes and geysers spout nitrogen gas.
*   8 moons (Triton, largest moon, at –235°C is coldest known thing in solar system).
*   Several rings around it.

1 Supply the following from this unit.

a) The main difficulty in gathering data about the large outer planets such as Jupiter and Saturn

_____

b) What happened between 1979 and 1989 that made it easier for scientists to study the outer planets.

_____

c) The name of the probe dropped on Saturn's largest moon. _____

2 Name or draw 1 characteristic you can see for each of the outer planets that will help you to remember that planet's name.

Jupiter	Saturn	Uranus	Neptune

3 Fill out the chart.

Planet			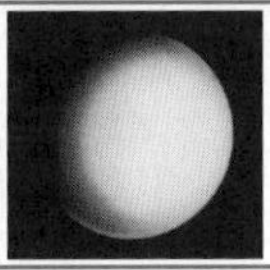	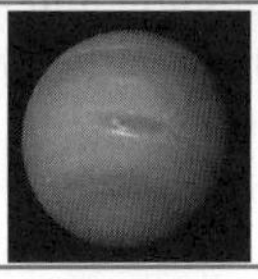
Name of planet				
Year Voyager 2 passed				
Temperature				
Main gas in atmosphere				
Moons				

4 Give 3 similarities between Jupiter and Saturn.

a) _____

b) _____

c) _____

5 Suggest reasons why it is unlikely that people will ever live on any of the outer planets.

_____

_____

6 Write down 3 things you have learned from this unit.

a) _____

b) _____

c) _____

7 Write down anything you need to ask your teacher to explain.

UNIT 30 SATELLITES

A **satellite** is any object that orbits a planet, moon or sun. Natural satellites are things such as Earth's moon or Jupiter's 39 moons.

Artificial satellites are man-made spacecraft. The first satellites were launched by carrier rocket engines or launch vehicles that fell back to Earth once the satellite was in orbit. More recently, satellites have been launched by reusable 'space shuttles'.

Artificial satellites travel around Earth in one of 3 orbits:

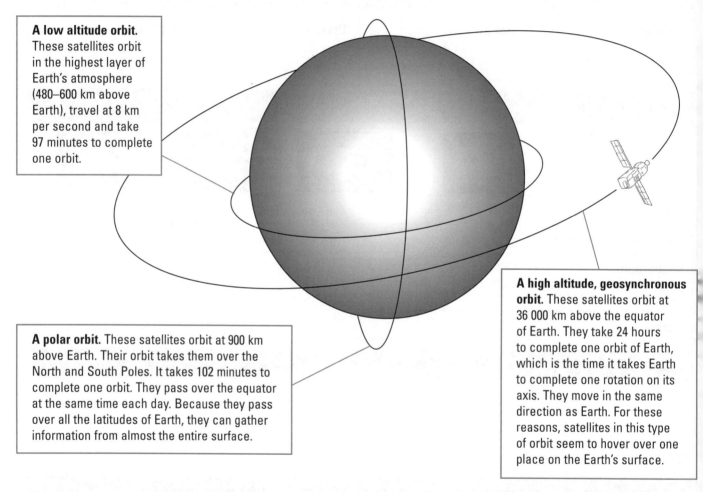

A low altitude orbit. These satellites orbit in the highest layer of Earth's atmosphere (480–600 km above Earth), travel at 8 km per second and take 97 minutes to complete one orbit.

A polar orbit. These satellites orbit at 900 km above Earth. Their orbit takes them over the North and South Poles. It takes 102 minutes to complete one orbit. They pass over the equator at the same time each day. Because they pass over all the latitudes of Earth, they can gather information from almost the entire surface.

A high altitude, geosynchronous orbit. These satellites orbit at 36 000 km above the equator of Earth. They take 24 hours to complete one orbit of Earth, which is the time it takes Earth to complete one rotation on its axis. They move in the same direction as Earth. For these reasons, satellites in this type of orbit seem to hover over one place on the Earth's surface.

More than 2 000 artificial satellites are orbiting Earth. They are grouped according to what job they do. The main groups are:

- **Communications (or Comsats)** Relay radio signals from one place to another. Signals may be television programmes, telephone calls or navigation signals from planes and ships. Usually in high altitude orbit over ground station.

- **Earth observation** Example is Landsat. Use visible light and infrared to take photographs of Earth's surface. Map and monitor Earth's resources, can identify sources of pollution, locate mineral deposits and fresh water. Use a polar orbit.

- **Military** Sometimes called 'spy satellites'. Detect movement of troops on ground, ships on sea and missiles launched. Use polar orbits so can observe entire surface of Earth. Military also use them for weather, communication and navigation purposes.

- **Navigation** Allow planes, ships, vehicles and people to know exact location. Global Positioning System (GPS) uses navigational satellites and can tell object's position on Earth within 10 metres. See Unit 31 for how GPS works.

A spy satellite in Earth orbit.

- **Scientific research** Gather scientific data about space near Earth (placed in different orbits), changes in Earth and its atmosphere (in polar orbits) and planets and stars in distant space (low altitude orbits). Hubble Space Telescope is satellite that orbits 610 km above Earth and produces very clear pictures of space beyond Earth because there is virtually no atmospheric dust to blur images. Information collected by instruments on Hubble Telescope gives chemical composition of stars and galaxies.

- **Weather** Gather information about weather patterns to help forecasters. Some (in polar orbits) measure things like temperature, air pressure and rainfall. Others (in high altitude orbits) photograph cloud formations and use infrared to measure heat being radiated from Earth. They can detect distress signals from planes and ships.

Weather satellites like this (above) provide weather forecasters with a stream of atmospheric images (below).

The Space Shuttle carries some satellites into orbit. Rockets, that fall into the sea once they have run out of fuel, launch others. Small thrusters on the satellites move them into the correct orbit. Earth's gravity holds them there. Solar panels use light energy from the sun to produce electrical energy to keep the satellite working. A control centre on Earth gives directions to the satellite when necessary and can sometimes repair and reprogramme the satellite if something goes wrong.

Satellites that cannot be repaired or can no longer do their job are shut down. They stay in orbit or they may slow down enough to be pulled into Earth's atmosphere where they burn up.

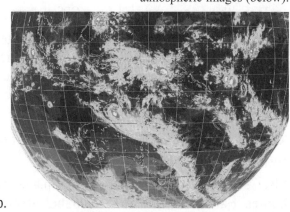

4U2DO

1 Give the difference between a natural satellite and an artificial satellite.

_____

2 Give reasons for the following.

a) The Hubble Space Telescope gives clearer pictures of objects in outer space than does a telescope on Earth

_____

b) Some satellites burn up _____

c) Rockets fall into the sea _____

d) High altitude satellites appear to hover over one place on Earth _____

_____

3 Write down 3 things you have learned from this unit.

a) _____

b) _____

c) _____

4 Write down anything you need to ask your teacher to explain.

_____

31 GPS – GLOBAL POSITIONING SYSTEM

GPS is a navigation system that uses radio waves sent out by 24 'Navstar' satellites in 6 different orbits above the earth. They are controlled by the US Air force. Navstar stands for Navigation Satellite Tracking and Ranging.

GPS is used to find out:

- your position on Earth (accurate to within 10m)
- your altitude
- your speed and direction of travel
- the time (where you are).

Three things are required for a GPS system:

'Space segment' or transmitter. 4 Navstar satellites in each of 6 orbits evenly spaced out around Earth. The satellites transmit constantly on 2 frequencies in microwave L-band that can penetrate cloud, rain, smoke dust and air pollution. 3 signals are sent out – one for military users, one for civilian users and one for all users (message saying where satellite is and that it is operational).

'Control segment'. Military base on Earth that calculates satellite's position and makes sure it is working properly.

'User segment'. GPS receiver in ship, plane, and car or held in hand of tramper or hunter. Hand-held receivers could be either Navigational (basic GPS features) or Mapping (have a few extra features such as greater memory).

GPS receivers calculate your position by measuring distances to at least four satellites and by using some geometry. These diagrams show, using 2D, how 3 satellites can locate you, using what is called triangulation.

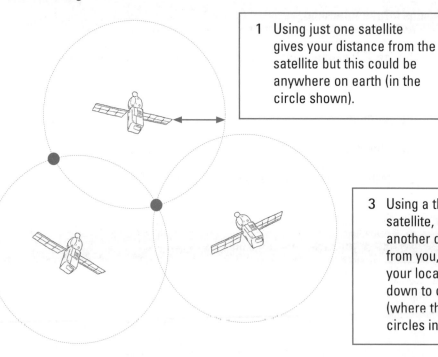

1 Using just one satellite gives your distance from the satellite but this could be anywhere on earth (in the circle shown).

2 Using a second satellite at a different distance from you, narrows down where you are to one of two points (where the two circles intersect).

3 Using a third satellite, at yet another distance from you, brings your location down to one point (where the three circles intersect).

These three measurements give your latitude, longitude and altitude. A fourth deals with the time the signals take to travel between your receiver and the satellites and the fact that the two do not have the exact same time. This fourth improves the accuracy of the data. Satellites use an atomic clock and receivers have a quartz crystal clock.

GPS was originally designed for military use but is now used in a wide range of ways. Here are some examples:

- **Emergency services** Police, fire and ambulance control centres can track all their vehicles and send the one that is closest to a burglary, fire or accident.

- **Lost pets** Digital implants in family pets track the pets and also monitor heart rate and temperature.

- **Personal emergencies** Strapped to the body, these systems can summon help in a medical emergency when the person cannot get to a phone.

- **Pest management** In northern Wairarapa tiny receiver/transmitters are attached to individual wild goats so they will lead hunters to larger goat populations which can be destroyed.

- **Helping the visually-impaired** 'Trekker' has been developed in Canada to 'talk' to visually-impaired people, telling them where they are and pointing out nearby attractions such as restaurants and museums.

- **Environmental monitoring** GPS-equipped balloons monitor the hole in the ozone layer over Antarctica. Large oil spills are tracked using buoys with GPS transmitters.

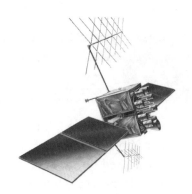

GPS satellite.

1 Give answers for the following.

a) What does GPS stand for? _____

b) What does Navstar stand for? _____

c) What information can you get using GPS? _____

_____

d) What 3 pieces of equipment are needed for GPS to work? _____

_____

e) What are the advantages of emergency vehicles using GPS? _____

_____

f) Find out any other uses for GPS apart from those in this unit. _____

2 Write down 3 things you have learned from this unit.

a) _____

b) _____

c) _____

3 Write down anything you need to ask your teacher to explain.

_____

_____

UNIT 32 | SPACE TRAVEL – LIVING IN SPACE

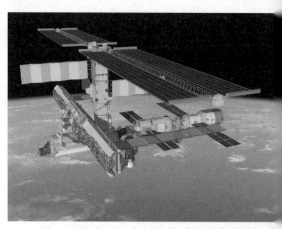

Astronauts have orbited Earth in spacecraft, lived and worked in space stations that orbit Earth, travelled to the moon and in July 1969 walked on the moon for the first time.

16 countries are combining their efforts to build the International Space Station (ISS). Astronauts from around the world will be able to live in it for extended periods and conduct experiments including growing protein crystals for cancer research, growing plants in micro gravity and studying the effects of micro gravity on the human body.

Scientists believe that in the next 20–30 years people could be living on the moon and there will be manned space flights to Mars.

International Space Station

Living and travelling in space exposes astronauts to many dangers. These include:

- **Extremes of temperature.** At 354km above Earth, the ISS is exposed to temperatures from 120°C to −155°C. Heat shields made of graphite and graphite composites are used to cover and protect the spacecraft and a cooling system inside keeps the temperature under control.

- **High levels of radiation.** One day in space exposes astronauts to the same amount of radiation they would get in a year on earth. Window filters stop harmful UV rays coming in. The white space suits reflect radiation while layers within the suit absorb or reflect gamma and x-rays. Astronauts also take large doses of vitamins A and C because these vitamins help protect the body from ultra-violet radiation.

- **Space junk.** A piece of paint the size of a full stop hit and dented a window in the Space Shuttle in 1983. There are over 100 000 man made objects orbiting the Earth as well as 'space junk' such as empty fuel tanks. Double-hulled spacecraft reduce the damage from such impacts.

- **Physical affects on their bodies.** Weightlessness or micro gravity can cause Space Sickness which is a kind of travel sickness. This nausea could be due to the inner ear not being able to sense the direction of movement and therefore shutting down while the eyes are sending messages to the brain saying you are moving. Medication can control the sickness and the inner ear starts working properly again once back on Earth. Loss of muscle tone including heart muscle occurs because there is no gravity to act against. Astronauts must exercise for 2 hours each day using treadmills, rowing machines, bicycles and rubber cords to provide the resistance needed to keep muscles working properly. Loss of minerals and weakening of bones is due to lack of stress on the bones. It is estimated that on a 9-month mission to Mars up to 45% of a person's bone mass could be lost. Exercise and dietary supplements can reduce the harmful effects.

While living and travelling in space, astronauts need their everyday needs met. These include:

- **Breathing.** There is no air in space so an air supply or means to make oxygen is needed. On the ISS some oxygen is stored and some is made by electrolysis of water. Some of the carbon dioxide produced is released into space and some is combined with hydrogen to produce water (reused) and methane (released into space).

- **Eating and drinking.** Food can be dehydrated or snap frozen and spacecraft have facilities to rehydrate and heat food. Water is recycled and reused. The ISS water recycling system reclaims water from fuel cells, urine, oral hygiene and hand washing and cabin humidity. This includes urine and breath produced by lab animals on the station. The system produces ultra pure water, far cleaner than tap water.

- **Getting rid of body wastes.** In the system used on the ISS an air suction under a toilet-like seat removes solid waste into a storage area. Urine is collected and recycled into water and oxygen.

- **Sleeping.** Sleeping bags strapped to the walls are used. Once inside, the astronauts are strapped in around their middles and have their arms in loops to stop them floating out in front of them. Often their 'biological clock' gets disrupted and their bodies' production of melatonin (sleep promotion) and cortisol (wakefulness promotion) hormones means they wake frequently and do not sleep as long as they would on Earth.

4U2DO

1   Give a piece of evidence to back up each of the following.

a) **ISS is an international project** _____

b) **The ISS aims to benefit mankind** _____

2   Fill out the chart.

Type of danger facing people in space	What is done to lessen the danger

3   Write down 3 things you have learned from this unit.

a) _____

b) _____

c) _____

4   Write down anything you need to ask your teacher to explain.

_____

33 SPACE SPIN-OFFS

A spin-off is something that has resulted from experiments, inventions or technology related to space travel and living in space. The use of space spinoffs in every aspect of our daily lives gives us an improved lifestyle.

All the examples here use materials or technology originally developed for the space programme.

Bar coding was developed to help keep track of millions of spacecraft parts. People who sell things use bar codes so they can keep track of what has been sold and what has not been sold.

Ear thermometers have a lens like a camera and detect infrared energy that we feel as heat. The warmer someone is, the more infrared energy they produce. This technology was originally developed to detect the birth of stars.

Smoke detectors were originally used on the Skylab space station to detect poisonous vapours. They are now used in homes to warn of fires.

Ski boots can be made with 'accordion-like folds', to allow the boot to flex without distortion but still provide support for your feet. These 'folds' were designed for use in space suits.

Invisible braces use brackets made of a see-through ceramic material that came from research into tough new materials for spacecraft and aircraft. The braces are nearly invisible.

Joystick controllers are used for such things as computer games and vehicles for people with disabilities. The joysticks were developed to control the Apollo Lunar Rover.

Aerodynamic bicycle wheels have 3 large spokes on the wheel which are the result of research into airfoils (wings). They make a bike more efficient for racing.

Miniaturised heart pump, battery-operated and only 5cm long and less than 50g weight can be implanted into a human heart to keep it pumping, perhaps while the patient waits for a transplant. It was originally designed as a fuel pump for use in the Space Shuttle.

MRI (Magnetic Resonance Imaging) is digital imaging that allows us to produce pictures of our insides. It was developed as a way of getting clearer images from spacecraft.

Digital Imaging Breast Biopsy System uses a digital camera system and a large core needle as a non-surgical way of detecting cancerous tumours. It is less painful than surgical biopsy and reduces scarring and exposure to radiation. The technology was developed for the Hubble Space Telescope.

Ribbed swimsuit has a thin layer applied to the swimsuit with 'riblets' that have small, barely visible grooves to reduce friction and drag by modifying the water flow next to the skin. It was originally designed to improve fuel efficiency in aircraft.

Whale studies use a NASA/French Space Agency Satellite that produces topographic maps showing the ocean currents speeds and direction where whales are feeding so research ships can move to those areas.

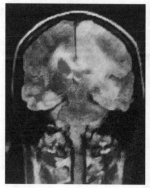

1 In the top boxes put the original space use and in the bottom boxes put the the spin-off uses on Earth.

2 Research some more space spin-offs and write a brief summary of one that interests you. Include a picture and explain why it was developed for the space programme.

picture

summary

3 Write down 3 things you have learned from this unit.

a) _____

b) _____

c) _____

4 Write down anything you need to ask your teacher to explain.

_____

_____

astronomy the study of planets, moons, stars

atom the basic building block of matter

atomic number the number of protons in the nucleus of an atom

axis an imaginary line around which the Earth rotates

biodegradable can be broken down by decomposers

carbohydrate a food group that includes starches and sugars

carnivore a living thing that eats another living thing for food energy

catalyst something that speeds up a chemical's reaction without being used up in the process

chemical energy the energy held in the bonds between atoms in a chemical

chemical formula symbols that represent molecules and compounds; a form of chemical shorthand

chemical reaction when chemicals combine to form new compounds

chemical symbol shorthand code for chemical elements

chromatography a technique for separating a mixture of gases, liquids, or dissolved substances

combustion when a substance burns, requires oxygen

compound a substance in which the atoms of different elements are chemically combined

conductor something that allows heat or electricity to pass through it

crystallisation forming crystals by cooling or evaporating a solution

dehydrate removing water from something so it dries out

dialysis tubing plastic tubing with very small pores to make it semi-permeable

digestive enzyme a chemical catalyst that helps break down complex food molecules into simple ones

distillate the liquid produced by distillation

distillation method used to separate or purify a mixture of liquids using evaporation and condensation

dry ice solid carbon dioxide

efficiency how much of the energy put into a machine is transformed into useful energy

elastic energy the energy stored in a squashed spring or a stretched piece of elastic or rubber

electrical energy the energy associated with electrons flowing through a conductor

electron negatively charged particles in an atom that move around the nucleus

electrolysis splitting a chemical compound using an electric current

element pure substance made up of only one type of atom

elliptical pathway the pathway in which the planets orbit the sun

energy something that 'does work'

equator an imaginary line that circles the middle of Earth dividing it into two halves or hemispheres

filtrate the liquid collected after it has passed through filter paper

filtration method that separates an insoluble substance from a liquid

first quarter when the moon is a quarter of the way through a month and appears as a half moon (semicircle)

fossil fuel formed from the remains of dead plants and animals

fractional distillation separating a mixture of liquids with different boiling points

fuel a form of stored chemical energy

galaxy a vast collection of stars

geosynchronous orbit a high altitude orbit, 36 000 km above Earth

glowing splint test test for oxygen gas; if the gas is oxygen, the splint re-ignites

gravitational energy the energy an object has when raised above the ground

gravity a force of attraction between two masses

'greenhouse effect' gases such as carbon dioxide in the atmosphere trapping infra-red radiation

heat a form of energy that affects the temperature of an object by making its particles move faster

herbivore animal that eats only plant material

ignite start to burn

infra-red radiation a form of electromagnetic radiation with a wavelength longer than red but shorter than radio waves

ion an atom that has gained or lost electrons

joule unit of energy

kilojoule 1000 joules

kinetic energy energy that a moving object has

last quarter when the moon is three-quarters of the way through a month and appears as a half moon (semicircle)

law of conservation of energy says energy cannot be created or destroyed but can be transformed from one form into another

light form of energy, part of electromagnetic spectrum

light year the distance that light travels in a year, 9.46 million million km

lipid food group that includes the fats and oils

low earth orbit orbit path 400 km above Earth

lunar month the time for a complete set of moon phases – 29.5 days

mineral salts chemicals containing elements needed in the diet

mixture a physical rather than chemical combination of substances

molecule a group of atoms joined together; the smallest part of a chemical compound that can take part in a reaction

moon a natural satellite that orbits a planet

neap tide a lower than normal high tide produced because the sun and the moon are at right angles to each other

neutron a particle found in the nucleus of an atom that has no charge; it is neutral

nuclear energy energy released as a result of nuclear fission (splitting a nucleus) or nuclear fusion (joining of nuclei)

nucleus the heavy central part of an atom made up of protons and neutrons

orbit the path of a planet around the sun or a moon around a planet

ozone layer layer of gas in the upper atmosphere that absorbs ultra-violet light

Periodic Table a list of all the chemical elements

petroleum oil a liquid mixture of hydrocarbons found in Earth's crust

phases of the moon the changing shape of the moon over a month as seen from Earth

planet a body that moves around a star e.g. Earth

plastics polymers that can be shaped by heat or pressure

pop test test for hydrogen gas, a flame causes the gas to explode with a 'pop' noise

potential energy energy that is stored

protein food group needed for growth and repair of cells

proton particle found in the nucleus of an atom that has a positive charge

radiant energy form of energy from the sun

radiation energy that travels through space as electromagnetic waves

reactants chemicals that take part in a chemical reaction

reaction a chemical combining of reactants to produce a new product or products

rust reddish-brown flaky material; iron oxide

satellite an object that orbits a planet

semi-permeable allows only some things to pass through it

solar system a group of planets and their moons orbiting a sun

sound a form of energy produced by vibrating objects

spring tide higher than normal high tide caused by the sun and moon pulling in same direction

star a ball of gases in which nuclear reactions are occurring

thermoplastics plastics that can be reused by reheating so they soften

thermosets plastics that cannot be reused because they will not soften on reheating

transferred energy moves from one object to another without changing form

transformed energy changed from one form to another

troposphere the lower layer of the atmosphere containing oxygen

universe all matter, energy and space that exists

vacuum space that contains relatively few atoms or molecules

vitamin chemicals essential for chemical reactions in the body

waste energy part of the input energy that has not been converted into useful energy by a machine

watt unit of power, rate of energy transformation; 1 watt = 1 joule/sec